and fauna. New developments in medicine interested him, too. When Boston was struck by a smallpox epidemic, Mather champi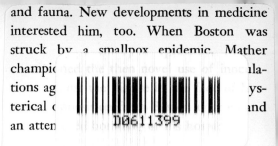ula-tions ag ys-terical (ind an atten

This book offers a strong portrait of Cotton Mather in the context of his time. It makes clear why the author feels Mather deserves the adjective "Admirable" before his name. It also complements Mr. Wood's earlier study of another important but little-understood figure from America's Puritan era, Jonathan Edwards.

The Admirable Cotton Mather

The Admirable Cotton Mather

by James Playsted Wood

THE SEABURY PRESS
NEW YORK

for E.C.W.

Preface

NO HISTORY of American thought can be complete without consideration of Cotton Mather.
Every serious anthology of American literature has to
include some of his writing. Cotton Mather was the
leading figure of his day in the Puritan church, history,
biography, science, medicine, and social reform. Yet
no man of the American past has been more consistently
derided.

". . . authorizing himself (for the most part) upon
other histories, whose greatest authorities are built upon
the notable foundations of hearsay . . . ," as Sir Philip
Sidney put it in 1595, the popular historian has car-
icatured rather than characterized Cotton Mather. He
has been established as a bigot, a reactionary, and the
villain of the infamous Salem witch trials of 1692.

It is always as easy as it is inaccurate to interpret a
man in terms of the ideas and prejudices of a later era
rather than in those of his own time—to take him out of

context, as it were. Some critics in the consciously enlightened mid-nineteenth century saw Puritanism, with
Mather its prime exponent, as narrow and contemptible
compared with their own wider understanding. The
much more self-consciously enlightened 1920's dis-
played its vaunted sophistication by derision of most
of the great men of the past; and Puritanism, with Cotton Mather an easy target, was anathema to what it
considered its complete moral and intellectual enfran-
chisement. Of course, neither the nineteenth century nor
the 1920's seem so enlightened now by comparison with
what we seem to feel our own ultimate understanding
of everything or a little more.

A changed attitude toward Cotton Mather began
with Professor Barrett Wendell's *Cotton Mather, the
Puritan Priest* in 1891. In their various writings George
Lyman Kittredge and Kenneth Ballard Murdock, also
of Harvard which was Cotton Mather's own "colledge,"
added to a better understanding of a vital and courageous
man, many of whose thoughts and actions show a sur-
prising resemblance to thought and action today. In
1953 two writers who examined the evidence bearing
on just one of his varied interests and accomplishments
could speak with justification of "the rediscovery of
Cotton Mather."

The attempt of this book is to give younger readers
a more just appraisal of Cotton Mather than he has oftentimes been accorded. For suggestions or research assist-

ance I am grateful to Dr. Donald M. Hobart of Hilton Head Island, South Carolina; Newton Felch McKeon, Director of the Robert Frost Library of Amherst College; Mrs. Joseph Withee of the City Library of Springfield, Massachusetts; Ethel L. Robinson of the Cleveland Public Library; and Katherine Smith of the Tracy W. McGregor Collection of the Alderman Library of the University of Virginia which now contains the William Gwynn Mather Collection of Matheriana. My thanks go always to Elizabeth Craig Wood.

J.P.W.

The Admirable Cotton Mather

One

COTTON MATHER'S name was Cotton Mather.

This startling revelation is not as silly as it sounds. His name was the basic fact of his early years, perhaps of the first half of his life. His maternal grandfather was the Reverend John Cotton. His paternal grandfather was the Reverend Richard Mather. His father, who was his almost lifelong associate and adviser, was the Reverend Increase Mather. There can be little understanding of Cotton Mather without some knowledge of the stature of these men in Puritan Massachusetts Bay who so deeply influenced him and whose mantle he felt he wore.

Born in Derbyshire, England, December 4, 1584, John Cotton was the son of a wealthy and very religious lawyer. The son took his B.A. degree at Trinity College, Cambridge, in 1603 and his M.A. in 1606. A natural scholar, he became dean and chief lecturer of Emmanuel College in Cambridge. During this period he was converted. He was ordained a deacon and priest of the Church of England in 1610 and took his divinity degree in 1613. At the age of twenty-seven he was made vicar of the large and important parish of St. Bodolph's in Boston in Lincolnshire.

Because he was a convinced Puritan, John Cotton omitted certain of the more elaborate forms and ceremonies from the liturgy of the English church. An assistant held services in St. Bodolph's in conformity with Church of England usage, but Cotton led a large part of his congregation into simpler Nonconformist ways. Insisting on return to what they considered the ways of the early Christian church, the Puritans disliked ceremony and what they believed wicked ostentation. Their ministers would not wear vestments. Puritan zealots in England's Boston even smashed all the beautiful stained glass windows in St. Bodolph's and defaced the monuments and carvings in the church.

Perhaps partly in sympathy with the views of his scholarly and brilliant priest, Cotton's bishop was lenient. He allowed Cotton to go his way unmolested. As a friend of John Winthrop's, Cotton went to Southampton in March 1630 and delivered a farewell sermon to those Puritans who—with the royal charter establishing the colony of Massachusetts Bay under their own almost independent direction—were setting sail for America. Three years later Cotton was summoned to appear before the Court of High Commission which had been appointed to investigate and if possible stamp out dissension in the English church.

Instead of appearing as ordered, Cotton, who had spent twenty years at St. Bodolph's, fled to London. From there, where he was protected by friends, he resigned his parish by letter to the Bishop of Lincolnshire and, in July 1633, sailed from Southampton for New England. Little more than a month after landing in Boston in Massachusetts Bay with his second wife and his first son—born at sea, hence named Seaborn—he was made teacher, or senior pastor, of the First Church. Immediately, the Reverend John Cotton became a leader in both church and colonial affairs.

Essentially they were the same. Unlike England, Massachusetts Bay did not have a state church. Instead, it was a church state. The colony was founded first as a church; second, as a political institution. Though they had a charter from the crown, the real basis of the Puritans' government in New England was the covenant which determined men made with God and with each other.

Unlike the humbler Pilgrims of Plymouth, the Puritans, who sent an advance party under the stern John Endecott to found Salem in 1629 and then founded Boston the next year, were strong, numerous, and powerful. Many of them were men of wealth with Cambridge, sometimes Oxford, educations. About a thousand people—gentlemen and their retainers, farmers,

traders, mechanics, and their families—came in the
Puritan fleet in 1630. Even the titled aristocracy was
represented in Sir Richard Saltonstall and in the Lady
Arbella, sister of the Earl of Lincoln. The immigrants
brought their money, their belongings, and their almost
feudal society with them.

There were the leaders like Governor John Winthrop, Simon Bradstreet, and the tough Thomas Dudley; and there were the led, everybody else. Both
leaders and followers were led by their ministers. Massachusetts Bay was no ordinary colony. It was a Bible
Commonwealth. It was a New Jerusalem. It was a City
of God in the wilderness of North America, and John
Cotton held it in his iron-hard spiritual hand.

A Nonconformist in England, he was a strict con-
formist to the Puritan code established in New England.
He was the pure Puritan and almost a dictator. Whatever he preached became the law of the church, the
colony, or both. A hard worker and a ready writer, he
was the recognized head of the Congregational Church
—the Puritan church which was governed by its congregation and ruled by no hierarchy of king or pope,
cardinals, archbishops, bishops, and priests. The Reverend John Cotton insisted on the complete power of
the church and his own power as its acknowledged
head. He distrusted the common people, saying, "Democracy, I do not conceyve that ever God did ordeyne

as a fitt government eyther for church or commonwealth."

He took an active part in all religious controversy
and in the trial and banishment of both Roger Williams
and Anne Hutchinson. Yet, narrow and opinionated as
he was, he was in some ways surprisingly liberal. The
Reverend Roger Williams, founder, perforce of Rhode
Island, insisted that the magistrates had no authority
over men's souls. Cotton ruled that in the church state
of Massachusetts the magistrates had authority in religious as well as in civil matters. Williams demanded
that only those who renounced the Church of England
be admitted to the Puritan church. Cotton declared that
no such renunciation of loyalty was necessary. His rule
as head of the orthodox Congregational church in Boston was almost absolute.

By his second wife, Sarah Hawkridge Story, the
widow whom he married shortly before leaving England, John Cotton had six children. After his death this
wife married Richard Mather, and later his daughter
Maria married Mather's son, Increase. Thus, Increase
Mather married his stepsister, who became the mother
of Cotton Mather.

The first of his line to reach New England, Richard
Mather was Cotton Mather's other grandfather. Among
the Puritan clergy of the first generation in the colony

of Massachusetts Bay, Richard Mather was almost as important as John Cotton.

He was a product of Oxford rather than of Cambridge. Born in Lancashire in 1596, he was first a schoolmaster in Toxteth Park, which became part of Liverpool. Converted in 1614, he entered Brasenose College, Oxford, in 1618 but was recalled to become preacher in the Nonconformist Toxteth Park Chapel. He was ordained a minister of the Church of England but for his severe puritanical practices was brought before the authorities and suspended in 1633. Friends exerted pressure and this suspension was revoked, but it was put in force a second time after another investigation of his conduct in the church. Richard Mather knew that John Cotton and Thomas Hooker, whose principles he shared, had already emigrated to New England and why. In 1635 he sailed from Bristol with his family. The next year he was made teacher of the church in Dorchester, just outside Boston, of which it is now a part. He remained in this pastorate until his death in 1669 when his grandson, Cotton Mather, was six years old.

He was a strong-voiced preacher and a practical church politician who worked for the immovable establishment of the Congregational Church in New England. With the Reverend John Eliot ("Apostle to the Indians") and the Reverend Thomas Weld, he translated the Psalms into English metre for singing in the church service. The *Bay Psalm Book*, issued from the press of Stephen Daye in Cambridge, was the first real book printed in America.

Like John Cotton, Richard Mather spent long hours each day in his study and in rapt devotion. He wrote almost a score of books in what was then virtually a coastal settlement on the frontier, for the unknown wilderness began not far west of Boston. In 1639 he wrote his *Church Covenant and Church Discussed*, a basic statement of the principles of the Congregational Church in Massachusetts Bay. In 1646 a convention of ministers appointed the Reverend John Cotton, the Reverend Ralph Partridge, and the Reverend Richard Mather to draw up a model platform of church government based on the Scriptures. It was the platform drawn up by Richard Mather which the convention adopted when it met again in Cambridge in 1648. The only manual the church ever accepted, this was the orthodox statement of rules for Congregational churches for more than one hundred years. Richard Mather's platform went through at least twenty-five editions.

Between them, Cotton Mather's two grandfathers did much to form and establish the Puritan Church in New England. In a sense, it was theirs. They had made it, and through them their grandson shared deeply in what they had created. He thought this and he felt it deeply. Beyond dispute, he knew in mind, heart, and soul that the Puritan Church was his. He felt that it was his duty and his destiny to keep the Congregational Church intact as it had been given him to hold and to lead. He had only to look at his father, whom he loved and reverenced, to feel even more blood certain.

That father was the greatest man, the most important and influential in the church and in the government of the New England colonies of his day and generation. Born in Dorchester, June 21, 1639, he was named Increase because of the great increase of all kinds in Massachusetts Bay. Had he been given, as was more usual, a Hebrew instead of an English name, it would have been Joseph, which means the same thing.

Increase Mather was brought up in the strict ministerial household of his father in Dorchester and educated at home and in the Boston schools. He learned Latin and Greek early and entered Harvard College when he was twelve years old, but he was taken out after a year because of ill health and sent to study with the Reverend John Norton. His illness brought on thoughts of death and damnation. Thirteen-year-old Increase Mather felt that he had somehow committed the unpardonable sin, but he was reassured by his father and, in an emotional experience which the Puritans understood and valued, was converted and brought to complete dependence on Christ for his salvation.

Increase Mather graduated from Harvard in 1656. On her deathbed his mother exhorted him to enter the ministry. There is little likelihood that he would have done anything else. On his eighteenth birthday in 1657 he preached his first sermon. He preached his second the next week in his father's pulpit. Less than a month later he left Dorchester and Boston for England, where his older brothers, Samuel and Nathaniel, were already established as preachers.

All England was Puritan now after the civil wars, the execution of Charles I, and establishment of the Commonwealth and then the Protectorate under Oliver Cromwell. There had been continual emigration of English Nonconformists to New England until 1640. Now many Puritans could and did return to England.

Increase Mather left Boston July 3, 1657, reached London after a voyage of five weeks, then went on to Liverpool, thence to Dublin in Ireland. His brother there looked after him like a father when he got first the measles, then smallpox. Despite these serious illnesses, Increase Mather took his M.A. degree at Trinity College, June 24, 1658. His scholarship and wit were so evident in his commencement address that to his surprise, for the compliment was not a custom in Massachusetts Bay, he was publicly hummed.

The young scholar was asked to stay on at Trinity as a Fellow, but the Irish climate did not agree with him, so he returned to England. For four months he was a minister at Great Torrington in Devonshire. From there he went to the Isle of Guernsey where he preached at the castle of the garrison every Sunday morning and in the town in the afternoon. He left Guernsey to preach in the cathedral city of Gloucester, but returned to the island when he saw the Restoration and the return of Charles II to the English throne coming. He was offered a good living in the Church of England in Dorsetshire, but, though he liked life in England, Increase Mather would not compromise his Puritan principles. He sailed from Weymouth for Newfoundland late in June 1661 and, after a long voyage, reached Boston September 1. He had been away a little over four years.

His arrival was unexpected. His family was delighted, particularly pleased because a brother, Eleazar, had just come home from his ministry in the remote Connecticut Valley. The next day the Reverend Richard Mather heard both his sons preach in his Dorchester church. Quickly, twelve churches offered their pulpits to the brilliant, highly educated, and widely traveled young Increase Mather. He delayed acceptance while he assisted his father in Dorchester, then chose to become teacher of the Second Church, the new church in the northern part of Boston. In March 1662 he married his stepsister Maria Cotton, and their first child, Cotton Mather, was born February 12, 1663.

Cotton Mather was fifteen months old when his father was ordained teacher of the Second or North Church, May 16, 1664. The elder Mather went on to achieve fame as a preacher and writer, as the acknowledged head of the Congregational Church in New England, as Fellow, then Rector, then President of Harvard College—and as its successful representative to the English court at a critical period in the history of Massachusetts Bay.

Two

COTTON MATHER was born to the Puritan purple. His grandfather Cotton, dead only a few years, had been virtually canonized by the early Puritans. His grandfather Mather was a small, bearded man with a ruddy complexion who preached in a loud, strong voice, a famous man who lived the life of a scholarly ascetic. His young father was both the hard student and early in his career the voice of the church in New England. His strong example in a home of stringent piety was before Cotton Mather from his first childhood.

When he was not abroad or away from home on his varied business of church and state, Increase Mather read a chapter of the Bible and prayed when he arose in the morning. He read or wrote until nine o'clock when he came downstairs for family prayers and breakfast, then returned to his study until midday dinner. He spent the afternoon and evening in his study, coming down for family prayers at nine o'clock in the evening, after which he often read or wrote until midnight. Usually Increase Mather spent nearly sixteen of the twenty-four hours in his study. He said that he would be content to stay in it all week, leaving it only to preach.

Though some in his parish complained, Increase Mather seldom made pastoral calls. His assistant could do that. Study and preaching were what he considered his mission. It was said of him that *"He never preach'd a Sermon, but what was worthy of the Press,"* and his sermons were plain and concise. According to his son, "He despised what they call *Quaintness* of Style; never had any Jingles of Words, nor any fanciful Turns of Thought; much less any of those tall Metaphors, that set the Rabble's gaping and raise Pity in the judicious part of the Auditory. . . ."

Grave and deliberate as he spoke, Increase Mather used no notes. He wrote his sermons in quarto notebooks, then memorized them. Though he kept a page or two of texts and hints in the opening pages of his Bible, he considered it a weakness to look at them. Increase Mather struck awe in the pulpit. In private conversation he was relaxed and easy—and never indecent, even, his son says, when he talked with "Persons of the First Quality," who evidently indulged in liberties of speech not permitted lesser men. Always he gave 10 percent of his income to charity. Any gratuities he received for preaching in other churches, and later his salary as Harvard president, he gave to widows and orphans. He was not only a leading minister, but also a man of mark in Boston. Like his father before him and his son after him he observed many private fasts and vigils.

At home, Increase Mather was gentle and kind. He loved his wife and his children. In time there were nine of them: Cotton, Nathaniel, Maria, Elizabeth, Sarah, Samuel, Catherine, Hannah, and Abigail. Infant mortality was high, but only one of the Mather children, Catherine, died in childhood. The Mathers were a strong family.

Their home, in which they lived for eight years, had been the home of John Cotton, and Cotton Mather's mother had been born in it. A double house near Pemberton Square, the southern half had been occupied by Sir Harry Vane, governor of Massachusetts Bay in 1636, and the northern by John Cotton and his family. Increase Mather may have had the entire house, which was spacious and well furnished with its china, pewter, tall chests of drawers, wall clock, and silver tankards. There was always good wine and beer in Puritan homes, and in this one there were as well many books, perhaps the largest library in Massachusetts Bay. Increase Mather himself is credited with writing and publishing one hundred and two sermons, books, and pamphlets, most of them dealing with religious and public questions of the time.

In such an environment Cotton Mather's tastes and habits were formed early. From the first he was very close to his father, and he had the unusual intelligence and nervous intensity of temperament which made him conform quickly and willingly to the pattern he knew.

The boy was precocious. Taught at home and in the Boston Latin School, he was the brilliant pupil of Ezekiel Cheever, early Boston's most famous schoolmaster. By the time he was twelve years old Cotton Mather had read Cicero, Terence, Ovid, and Virgil in Latin. He had read the New Testament in Greek and begun to read Homer and Socrates. He was studying Hebrew grammar. Said to be the youngest student ever admitted up to that time, he entered Harvard, of which his father had been made a Fellow in 1674.

Cotton Mather is said to have undergone some mild hazing by his fellow students, kind unspecified, but this could hardly have deterred him. He was a natural student, and he was early convinced that, like his father and grandfathers, he was destined to lead the Congregational Church. Yet in college he showed a definite interest in science and began the study of medicine. He feared that his stammering, which had affected him from childhood, would prevent his entering the ministry and thus he determined to become a physician.

Cotton Mather graduated from Harvard in 1678. At his graduation a brilliant future was forecast for him.

In all the solemnity of his Latin oration at commencement President Urian Oakes recognized his eminent ancestry and singled him out for especial praise. As his words were translated by the Reverend Abijah O. Marvin in *The Life and Times of Cotton Mather, D.D., F.R.S.*, President Oakes said:

Mather is named Cotton Mather. What a name! My hearers, I mistake; I ought to have said what names! I shall not speak of his father, for I dare not praise him to his face. But should he resemble his venerable grandfathers, John Cotton and Richard Mather, in piety, learning, splendor of intellect, solidity of judgment, prudence, and wisdom, he will indeed bear the palm. And I have confidence that in this young man Cotton and Mather will be united to flourish again.

For a time Cotton Mather devoted himself to teaching. He taught his younger brothers, Nathaniel and Samuel, and probably his sisters, Maria, Elizabeth, and Sarah, as well as a few other pupils. He prayed hard that he be cured of the impediment in his speech. To his prayers he added his own strong effort.

Demosthenes, statesman and orator of Athens in the fourth century B.C., is reputed to have cured himself of stammering by filling his mouth with pebbles and trying to make himself heard above the roar of the sea. He shouted declamations as he ran uphill. Cotton Mather did not use such strenuous methods, but he took sound advice and exerted all the force of his unusual will. While he was most concerned about the affliction which threatened his career before it had started, one of his old schoolmasters, Elijah Corlet, paid him a purposeful visit. According to Mather's son, Corlet said, *"Sir, I should be glad if you would oblige yourself to a* dilated Deliberation *in speaking; for as in singing there is no one who* stammers, *so by prolonging your* Pronunciation *you will get an habit of speaking without Hesitation."*

In all probability Cotton Mather's tongue had been unable to keep pace with his rapid mind and in his eagerness he had been trying to talk too fast. He slowed his speech, forcing himself to the deliberate expansion in forming his words which Corlet had suggested. His efforts were successful and Cotton Mather ceased to stammer. He never ceased to thank God that he who had been a "great *Stammerer*" became a skilled preacher and public speaker.

Cotton Mather had no hesitation now in entering the ministry. February 23, 1680, the North Church unanimously invited him to become assistant to his father.

August 22, 1680, Cotton Mather preached his first sermon in what had been his Mather grandfather's pulpit in Dorchester. The following Sunday he preached for his father in the Second Church. A week later he preached, as Samuel Mather phrased it, "at his other Grandfather's desk in Boston," that is, in the First Church. In 1681 Cotton Mather received from Har-

vard's most illustrious Fellow, Increase Mather, his
M.A. degree.

When Urian Oakes died, July 25, 1681, the presidency of Harvard, which had been founded in 1636 by
the first generation of Puritans, was immediately offered
to Increase Mather. Because he would have to leave them
to live in Cambridge, the congregation of the Second
Church objected to the Harvard Overseers, and Increase
Mather declined the office. John Rogers was then
chosen, but he died the day after commencement, July
2, 1684.

Cotton Mather tells the rest of the story in his history
of Harvard. "The college was now again, by universal
choice, cast into the hands of Mr. Increase Mather, who
had already, in other capacities, been serving of it; and
he accordingly, without leaving either his *house* or his
church in Boston, made his continual visits to the colledge at Cambridge, managing as well the weekly *dis-
putations*, as the annual *commencements*, and inspect-
ing the whole affairs of the society; and by preaching
often at Cambridge, he made his visits there yet more
profitable to them."

Increase Mather's title during his first tenure at Harvard was "rector." It was changed to "president" in
1692.

Before he was nineteen years old Cotton Mather was
offered the church in New Haven made famous as the

pastorate of John Davenport. The North Church demurred. It kept him on as assistant to his father at seventy pounds a year.

Religion was not an exterior adornment or mere formal protestation of Puritan life. It was its center. The Puritans held to the Bible and to direct access to God without intercession by saints or ecclesiastical authorities. They strained to know and do God's will, to know God, to identify themselves with him—and their ministers strove harder than the rest. Through prayer and fasting, through vigils and thanksgivings, through devotions that were a continual part of their days and nights, they tried to approach God and, like the medieval mystics, reach him in emotional transport.

In its essence Puritanism was not the grim and cold way of life depicted by the scornful critics of later centuries but a worship with fire at its heart. It was the devouring reality to Cotton Mather. In May 1681 he wrote in his diary:

This Day, I thus renewed my closure with the Lord Jesus Christ.

"Lord, I am a vile *Sinner*, and, which my Soul melts at the mention of, Thou are justly *angry* with mee. But, Oh! for a *Reconciliation*. Lord, *is there no hope in Israel?* Yes, thou hast opened a *Door of Hope*. And what a Word is that which thou has spoken? Thou dost even *beseech Sinners* to bee reconciled unto thyself. Is that so? Lord, I am willing to bee reconciled unto thee; my very Soul desires to love thee, and love thy Wayes, and walk therein always, even unto the End. But is there not a *Jesus* who *delivers from the Wrath to come?* A JESUS! Lord, my Soul now lives and melts at the remembrance of that sweet Name. A JESUS who is a *mighty Saviour.* To Him I go; and, Lord, it is at thy bidding that I go. It is Hee that *formerly* invited mee, *formerly* encouraged mee, *formerly* assisted mee, to come unto Him, and I *formerly* have also found it *good for mee* so to do. Hee calls even such as I am, and solemnly professes that Hee will not *cast them out,* when they *come* unto Him. Lo! then I come; I bring my Soul unto Him; Oh! Lett Him save mee. Is not Hee a *Priest, a Prophet, a king?* therefore Hee will be *All* to mee, and tho' my Distempers are so very strong, that I am in myself an utter Loss, how to releeve myself, yett Hee will be my Undertaker; I will *rejoice in that Lord, and in His Salvation.* Hee will carry on the works which Hee has begun, till the *Times of Refreshing* do come from the *Presence of the Lord.*"

It is all there: the faith, the self-abasement, the rapture, fear, love, and inexpressible yearning of the mystic. Even to its emotional incoherence, this is the Christian mystic straining for greater love and realization of God. Through fasting and prayer, through asceticism, he strives to know God in rapture. Essentially it was the same for St. Bernard, St. Catherine of Siena, St. Teresa —or John Cotton or Jonathan Edwards.

Cotton Mather may have been imitating any one of

them or his father, yet there is unmistakable sincerity
about his emotion and his devotion. There is also Puritan
or Calvinistic doctrine. Man is born in sin. In himself
he is nothing. He can be saved only through Jesus Christ
who died for the sins of men and through Christ reach
the godhead. Yet it is not quite that simple. The rapture,
the transporting sense of final union with God through
Christ, is inexpressible. It cannot be logically conveyed
in words. If it could be, it would not be mysticism—or
religion or poetry.

Cotton Mather wrote these words when he was eighteen years old, but what he felt and wrote was not sprung
of the enthusiasm of youth or the shrill wonder of the
recent convert. Using other words and phrases, sometimes the same ones, he wrote much the same thing at
fifty and at sixty and in all the years of his life. He
meant it. By temperament he was oversensitive and
agonizingly introspective, but he did not pose. Deeply,
as well as in his actions, he was a godly man.

In 1681 he listed too, as he did so many times later,
what he called the kindnesses of God to him. He may
have felt that he was singled out for leadership and
sainthood. He had a controlling pride of ancestry, position, and intellect, but he was never ungrateful.

1. How wonderful is the Goodness of God unto mee, a
vile Worm, in that Hee does employ mee, in the *Ministry*
of the glorious Lord Jesus Christ!

2. How *Miraculous* a Thing is the *Freedom of Speech* conferred upon mee, and enlarged unto mee, in most sensible Answers to many Prayers!

3. How mercifully has the Lord upheld *mee* in His work, notwithstanding my *weak Head*, and my *vain Heart*, which render mee the unfittest of most Men living for eminent Services!

4. How great and growing a *Reputation* has the Lord given unto mee, a most Contemptible Creature, among his People!

5. What comfortable *Provision* has the Lord made for mee, as to my temporal and saecular Condition; even to a Wonderment! . . .

Again and again Cotton Mather listed his blessings in innumerable private thanksgivings. In days of personal tragedy and bitter unhappiness he had to reach for them sometimes, but he found them.

If Increase Mather abstained from pastoral calls, his son did not. From the first, Cotton Mather took his ministry to his people. As early as 1681 he was visiting the poor and the sick. He prayed with debtors, thieves, pirates, and murderers throughout his ministry, often giving what comfort he could to men on their way to the gallows.

Cotton Mather was ordained pastor of the Second Church—associate of his father who was its teacher, or senior minister—May 15, 1685, when he was twenty-two years old. His father and the ministers of the First

Church and the South Church took part in the solemn ceremony. Ordinarily it would be the youngest minister present, but this time it was the Reverend John Eliot, now very old, who gave him the right hand of fellowship. That day, as he said, the young minister "went into one of the vastest congregations that has ever been seen in these parts of the world, and preached [on John 21:17] about an hour and three-quarters."

Thus Cotton Mather entered on his professional career in which he would be his father's confidant, ally, and champion for the next thirty-eight years. He would remain in the Second Church until he died.

A young minister was expected to marry, and Cotton Mather was soon very much in love. He prayed for guidance during his courtship and May 4, 1686 the crown prince of the Cotton and Mather dynasty and a prince of the Puritan Church married Abigail Phillips. She was the daughter of a prosperous merchant, loyal churchman, and militia colonel of Charlestown, just across Boston Bay.

For several months Mather and his bride lived with his father-in-law. Then they moved back to John Cotton's house in which Cotton Mather had been born. It was near the church, and his father, mother, brothers, and sisters lived just a few houses away. The Mathers' first child, Abigail, was born August 22, 1687, but died an infant. Cotton Mather, who loved his children as dearly as his father loved his, was deeply grieved. In a sermon of 1689 he said, "Of outward, earthly anguishes, none equal unto these. The dying of a child is like the tearing of a limb unto us." He had other grief. His promising younger brother, Nathaniel, died late in 1688, seemingly of exhaustion from overstudy.

Cotton Mather had need of fortitude early, and quickly now he needed all the skill and learning, all the force of character, he possessed. Less than two years after his marriage he was left in sole charge of the Second Church, one of the most important in New England. Every Sunday he preached to huge congregations. A scholar, a wit, his reputation already established, he was a pulpit idol. He spoke to audiences numbering about 1,500 people—at a time when the total population of Boston stood somewhere between 10,000 and 12,000.

Increase Mather was absent because there was a crisis in the affairs of Massachusetts Bay and all New England and in the affairs of the Congregational Church. From 1629 to 1684 Massachusetts governed itself under the terms of the charter which the English crown granted "The Governor and Company of the Massachusetts-Bay in New England." It was under this authority that John Winthrop, John Cotton, and their peers established and upheld the theocracy. On the Restoration in 1660 England demanded return of this charter. Massachusetts Bay demurred and delayed. Finally, in 1684, the Court of Chancery in England in-

validated the charter and appointed Joseph Dudley pro-
visional governor of the colony. In 1686 Sir Edmund
Andros was appointed royal governor of Massachusetts Bay, Plymouth, Maine, New Hampshire, and the
Narragansett Bay. Andros arrived in Boston with British frigates and all the panoply of British rule. Worse,
he brought with him priests of the Church of England
and instituted services of that dispensation in Boston.
Still worse, Andros declared that the colonists did not
own the land on which they had built their homes or
the farms they had cleared and worked. Everything was
the property of the British crown.

Massachusetts Bay was in an uproar. For more than
a half century its people had elected their own governors and representatives and made their own laws. They
had built their own church. Now they were subject to
what to many of them was a foreign country and to the
tyranny of outside rule. Desperately they wanted back
the charter which was Massachusetts' guarantee of freedom and practically its constitution. They sent their
strongest man to England to get it back.

Increase Mather was a Puritan priest, a scholar, and
the head of Harvard. He was also a diplomat of sound
and balanced judgment who, from his four years' resi-
dence there, knew England and the English. He left
Boston April 7, 1688, but he did not get away without
difficulty. From the first both Increase and Cotton
Mather had spoken and acted against the Joseph Dudley

and Andros governments. In 1684 Increase Mather had written a number of letters to a friend in Amsterdam. Enemies—and the outspoken Mathers always had plenty of them—somehow obtained the letters and could thus imitate his signature. Using it, Cotton Mather says, "They forg'd a letter full of impertinences, as well as treasonable expressions whereof not one sentence was his; and with a Date, Boston, 10 m 3 d, 1683, they subscrib'd his name to it. This letter was read before the King and Council. It was fear'd that it would have been his ruin. Mr. Mather was concerned to think that he was like to suffer as an Evil Doer. . . . But here it ought to be considered, that most, if not all the faithful ministers of Jesus Christ, are, or have been exposed to the vilest Reproaches, which wicked Men, Hypocrites, and Apostates, can call upon them."

Increase Mather was arrested and sued for five hundred pounds by a man whom he named as suspect in the forgery, but a jury cleared him, and the plaintiff was ordered to pay court costs. Another attempt was made to arrest him, but the arresting officer could not gain admittance to his house. As he was about to leave for England the rumor spread that he had been arrested again. To get away, Increase Mather had to take refuge in the home of his son's father-in-law in Charlestown. Agents of the Andros government even pursued the boat in which he was rowed to his ship, but he escaped and got safely aboard.

In England, Increase Mather went quickly and deftly to work. He enlisted the aid of court favorites—among them William Penn—in the cause of Massachusetts Bay. He was tactful in his audiences with James II, kneeling and kissing his hand. Realizing quickly that the original charter would never be returned, he did not ask it. Instead, he tried to get all the concessions he could written into a new one. He asked that liberty of religious conscience be established (a liberal request from the leader of a weakening theocracy), that titles to land be confirmed, and for the right of free assembly. He asked that Harvard remain under control of men who shared the principles of its founders. He had a half dozen audiences with James II, who promised affably that he would see to what Mather asked. Events moved too fast. James II was driven from the throne and fled to France. Prince William of Orange and his wife Mary, daughter of James II, were proclaimed king and queen of England, February 13, 1689.

After almost sixty years, Boston was no longer a disciplined Puritan village. It was a thriving seaport, the metropolis, as Cotton Mather described it, of New England. It had sailors, slaves, traders, pirates, as well as docile citizens. It had Quakers, Anabaptists, Presbyterians, and Episcopalians as well as orthodox Congregationalists. It had grog houses and dives as well as churches. When news of the revolution in England reached New England, Boston did not wait official notification. Militia raced in from the surrounding towns to join forces with the armed Boston crowd. The insurgents imprisoned Andros in his own fort and seized the British frigate in the harbor. They incarcerated Joseph Dudley, particularly hated because as son of Governor Thomas Dudley, one of the original Puritan leaders, he was viewed as a traitor. The king's minions deposed, Boston proceeded to govern itself again under what it considered the God-given rights of its old charter.

This violent action did not make Increase Mather's task easier. William III confirmed the royal colonial governors in their posts. Mather objected that this would keep in power rulers the people detested, so the king, though he pointed out that Massachusetts Bay had been irregular in performance of its duties to the crown, excepted it from his order. In introducing Mather at the court, Lord Wharton had explained that Massachusetts did not petition for money, troops, or any other aid but only for restoration of its ancient rights and privileges. William III, who wanted the aid of New England in prosecuting England's wars against France, was favorably disposed.

The House of Commons voted restoration of the Massachusetts charter, but the move failed. Again with Lord Wharton, but this time at Hampton Court, Mather now petitioned King William for a new charter which would restore all of the privileges lost in the old and add new ones. The Earl of Monmouth presented this petition personally to the king on Mather's behalf. While the king was absent in Holland, Mather worked with the Privy Council and pressed his suit with Queen Mary.

Diplomacy usually requires long periods of waiting as well as active maneuvering for a cause. Mather used the time when he was not actually engaged in his agent's duties to mingle with the statesmen, courtiers, and men of learning in England. He made friends with the Puritan divine and scholar Richard Baxter and with the physicist and inventor Richard Boyle. Boyle was one of the first members of the Royal Society of London for Improving Natural Knowledge, one of the world's first scientific bodies. In London, Increase Mather bought books on science and politics and published several pamphlets. His interests were wide. He came to know the antiquarian Anthony Wood; Wood disliked Puritans but liked Increase Mather. Mather helped form a plan for union of the Congregational and Presbyterian churches. Though *in absentia*, he was still head of Harvard, and he worked successfully to obtain bequests for it from wealthy Englishmen. Two senior tutors, John Leverett and William Brattle, were managing the college while he was abroad.

When the new Massachusetts charter was drawn up by England's Attorney General and Solicitor General,

Mather objected to some of its provisions, saying that "He would sooner lose his Life, than consent to that which could infringe any liberty or Privilege, that justly belonged to his Countrey." He managed to get some changes made in the charter, including confirmation of all grants which had been made by the Massachusetts General Court and removal of the rite of kissing the Book from the order for taking an oath.

Admired in England for his learning and his character, Increase Mather proved himself a statesman. He accomplished his mission. Three other Massachusetts agents, one of them Sir William Ashurst, had now joined him. They formed their own council. William III told Mather—introduced this time by the Earl of Nottingham—that he wished this council to nominate a man of their own choice for royal governor. Increase Mather nominated Sir William Phips, and the council agreed. In diplomatic language recorded by Cotton Mather in his life of Phips, Increase Mather presented his choice.

Sir William Phips has been accordingly nominated by us at the COUNCIL-Board. He hath done a good Service for the Crown, by enlarging your Dominions, and reducing Nova Scotia to your Obedience. I know that he will faithfully serve your Majesty to the utmost of his Capacity, and if your Majesty shall think it fit to confirm him in that place, it will be a further obligation on your subjects there.

The new charter obtained and a governor of his choice appointed, Increase Mather had done his job. "As Day and Night have seen it," he said, "so I can appeal to Heaven and Earth, that I have served the People of my Country with all Fidelity and to the utmost of my Capacity." Leaving his youngest son, who was ill of smallpox, in London, Mather and Sir William Phips sailed for home aboard a merchantman with a British man-of-war, the *Nonesuch*, for escort. After a long voyage in which they narrowly escaped capture by four French warships, ambassador and new royal governor reached Boston May 14, 1692.

Massachusetts Bay proclaimed a day of thanksgiving for the safe return of "His Excellency our Governour, and the Reverend Mr. Increase Mather, who . . . have industriously endeavoured in the Service of this People, and brought over with them a Settlement of Government; in which their Majesties have graciously given us distinguishing Marks of their Royal Favour and Goodness." Harvard advanced Increase Mather to its presidency.

His services advanced his stature, though there were those, of course, who found fault, for Increase Mather was now in the political arena as well as in the church. He was attacked for not getting the original charter back, for some of the terms of the new one, even for spending too much money. In a pamphlet retort to those whom his son scornfully described as "Silly Demagogues," Increase Mather rejoined, "These little Men know not what it is to attend in the Court of Kings for four Years together; if they did, they would not make that objection."

Three

D ESPITE his title, Sir William Phips was not born in England, and he was far removed from the hereditary aristocracy. He was a down-East Yankee from the Maine frontier, where he was born in 1651, and the very prototype of the American self-made man. A ship's carpenter, he moved to Boston where he plied his trade, married advantageously, became a shipbuilder and then a shipmaster. Suddenly he was a romantic hero and a rough and ready man of the world.

In 1684 he persuaded Charles II to equip him with a vessel, H.M.S. *Rose*, and sailed off to recover the wealth aboard a Spanish ship sunk off the Bahamas. The expedition failed, but Phips obtained new backing from a company headed by the Duke of Albemarle. This time he succeeded munificently. He recovered gold and jewels to the value of 300,000 pounds and took it triumphantly to England. Made wealthy by this exploit, he was knighted and appointed Provost Marshal of New

England. Phips was in Boston just after the overthrow of Andros and a partisan of the insurgents, of whom Cotton Mather was one.

While his father was in England, Cotton Mather was active in the same cause, recapture of Massachusetts' rights and re-establishment of the Congregational Church. Young as he was, as pastor of the Second Church he was in a dominant position and so outspoken in opposition to Andros that he was about to be arrested. The insurgents conferred with him before they moved on Andros and Dudley. He approved their planned action but warned against unnecessary violence. He was as close to Sir William Phips as his father was; perhaps closer, for the tie was churchly and thus social.

In 1690 Phips applied for membership in the Second Church. In the seventeenth century and well into the eighteenth admission to full membership in the Puritan Church could be granted only after the supplicant made public avowal of having been converted through personal religious experience. Phips made a long confession of faith and testament to his conversion which was read aloud to the congregation of the North Church. He started by saying that his religious consciousness had first been awakened by hearing Increase Mather preach in 1674. "Accordingly on March 23, 1690, after he had in the Congregation of North-Boston given himself up, *first unto the Lord, and then to his people*, he was Baptized and so received into the *Communion* of the Faithful there." It was Cotton Mather who wrote this, and it was Cotton Mather who baptized the first royal governor and admitted him to Communion.

In effect, Sir William Phips was the Mathers' man. He owed his hopes of everlasting life to the son and his royal governorship to the father. Through Phips the Mathers hoped to restore the Congregational Church to its former position of undisputed dominance in Massachusetts Bay. As John Cotton and, to a lesser extent, Richard Mather had been, they became in this way temporal as well as spiritual powers. Times had changed and changed radically between 1630 and 1692, but the Mathers hoped that they could keep one factor constant, their church and their leadership of it.

One of the results as well as one of the symptoms of the upset times had already manifested itself before Increase Mather and Sir William Phips returned. Cotton Mather had noted its appearance in his diary, May 14, 1692. "The Divels, after a most praeturnatural Manner, by the dreadful Judgment of Heaven took a bodily Possession of many people in Salem and the adjacent places; and the Houses of the poor People, began to be filled with the horrid Cries of Persons tormented by *evil Spirits*. There seem'd an execrable *Witchcraft* in the foundation of this wonderful Affliction, and many Persons of diverse Characters, were accused, apprehended, prosecuted upon the *Visions* of the Afflicted."

Almost everyone, high and low, educated and ignorant, believed in witchcraft in the seventeenth century, as people had believed for centuries before. The Devil and his agents were as real to them as God and his angels. In English law witchcraft was a capital crime, punishable by death. Thousands of condemned witches had been put to death in England, Scotland, Holland, France, and other countries of Europe. Philosophers, scientists, statesmen, and physicians all believed that witches existed and bedeviled their victims. Most eminent physician of his day, Sir Thomas Browne concurred without a murmur when Sir Richard Hale, Baron of the Exchequer, sentenced two women accused of witchcraft to death. Witches were executed under Oliver Cromwell just as they had been under Queen Elizabeth. Oftentimes torture was used to extract confessions and many of the forms of execution were gruesome. Joan of Arc was burned at the stake as a witch in 1431. Accused of spiriting away more than one hundred children and trying to force them into the community of the Devil, scores of witches were executed in Sweden in 1669 and 1670.

Not only English law, but the Bible—which the Puritans read literally—proclaimed the existence of witches and ordered their deaths. The Mosaic Law was specific. It read, Exodus 22:18, "Thou shalt not suffer a witch to live." Leviticus, 20:27 said: "A man also or a woman that hath a familiar spirit or is a wizard, shall surely be put to death." It was both lawless and irreligious not to believe in witchcraft and prosecute those who practiced it—a denial of the word of God. It was likewise impossible not to believe, for the evidence was to be found everywhere.

If a man had an epileptic child, he knew its seizures were caused by a witch. If his chimney fell or his house caught fire or his wife ran away or someone in the family came down with an unexplainable illness or his cow behaved strangely, he knew it was the work of witches. Everyone knew that witches met at night in the woods in the darkness of the moon and held seances with their master, Satan. None of this was superstition or fantasy in the seventeenth century. It was fact. There are people still who believe in witchcraft and references to older beliefs survive in colloquial speech. We speak of somebody's or something's being bewitched when an action baffles or a device does not operate properly.

In his *Cotton Mather, the Puritan Priest*, 1891, Barrett Wendell hazarded a conjecture which still makes sense. Disclaiming any scientific or expert knowledge, Wendell suggested that primitive man and man in earlier times had—perhaps had to have in order to survive —knowledge transcending that obtained through his senses. He suggested that remnants of this extrasensory knowledge may persist in man and sometimes cross the threshold into conscious awareness. He spoke of "Powers of perception which countless centuries of disuse had made so rudimentary that in our normal condition we are not conscious of them. But, if such were the case, it would not be strange that in abnormal states, the rudimentary vestiges of these disused powers of perception might sometimes be revived." In Wendell's opinion, witches, mediums, sorcerers, and the like actually do see in the world about us things that are not perceptible to normal human beings in their normal state. These people—thus the trance of the spiritualist—retrogress from high mental and moral levels to perception on a much lower level of animal awareness. Wendell's reasoning is plausible.

There were other factors in the outbreak of something unusual and the hysteria that gripped Salem—about fourteen miles north of Boston—in 1692.

Life was hard, lonely. There were few diversions, few emotional outlets, and the dark and forbidding wilderness was close. West Indian slaves brought their superstitions and perhaps their knowledge of voodoo into the region. There were many Indians, and many Indian slaves. The Puritans believed that before they came to New England, Satan had ruled the American continent and that the Indians were his people. When they spoke of the Indians as devils, they meant what they said literally. Old men and women, often neglected, sometimes eccentric, were viewed with fearful suspicion. If only to drive away boys who ridiculed or abused them, they sometimes retaliated by pretending to be witches and able to call down curses on the heads of their tormenters.

In almost every community there were those popularly known or suspected to be witches and in league with the Devil. Farmers would not drive past the houses of certain old women who they were convinced would bewitch their horses and perhaps them too. There had been isolated cases in Massachusetts Bay of women being tried for witchcraft. Mary Parsons had been accused of bewitching the children of the minister in Springfield in 1645. The poor, half-crazy woman was sent on to Boston where she was found guilty, but the General Court dismissed the case, and Goody Parsons is thought to have died in prison. In Boston in 1655 Mrs. Anne Hibbins, embittered and quarrelsome widow of an Assistant to the General Court and one of the colony's agents in England, was accused by her neighbors of witchcraft. She was censured by the church and found guilty by a jury. Again, the General Court reversed the decision, but renewed public clamor forced the Court to sentence her to death.

There had been these and perhaps a few other cases, but, in actuality, there had been fewer witch scares and witch trials in New England than in other countries. In no case was torture used to extract confessions. Neither was it used in Salem.

One other factor may have contributed to the outbreak there—and Cotton Mather thought it did. In the popular mind witchcraft has always been allied to magic, black magic, divination, fortune-telling, conjuring, sleight-of-hand, palmistry, and other mysterious signs and portents. There was a strong underground interest in these in Massachusetts Bay at this time. It had been renewed through books brought in from England and kept out of sight of magistrates and ministers.

Mather wrote, "It is to be confessed and bewailed, that many Inhabitants of *New-England*, and Young People especially, had been led away with little *Sorceries*, wherein they *did secretly those things that were not right against the Lord their God*; they would often cure Hurts with *Spells*, and practice detestable Conjurations with *Sieves*, and *Keys*, and *Pease*, and *Nails*, and *Horse-shoes*, and other Implements, to learn things for which they had a hidden and impious Curiosity."

The devils had been played with, he says. As a result, they broke out in a fearsome manner. Certainly they chose a place where the atmosphere and all the omens were propitious for their devilment. All the ingredients had been brought together in Salem Village (Danvers), a farming community which was a separate parish of Salem itself. Salem Village had long been notorious for its bickering, gossip, and acrimony. It had a habit of mistreating its ministers and then dismissing them. There were established feuds and animosities—and there were the Reverend Samuel Parris and a household of neurotic, vindictive, and irresponsible girls.

That is where it all started in the spring of 1692. Samuel Parris was not an ordinary minister. Leaving Harvard without finishing his course, he had gone to the Barbados as a trader and failed. By the time he was thirty-five he needed a job, and the ministry seemed profitable and secure. After a year of petty negotiation with the church in New Salem, he came to the difficult community on niggardly terms in 1689. With him he brought his family and two slaves, John Indian and Tibuta, said to be part Negro and part Carib Indian. The presence of the Parris' nine-year-old daughter Elizabeth and her cousin, eleven-year-old Abigail Williams, but especially of Tibuta, made the Parris parsonage a gathering place for a group of young girls aged up to twenty of Salem Village.

Tibuta entertained them with half-remembered voodoo rites and magic spells. When some of the suggestible girls showed symptoms of epileptic seizure, Tibuta claimed that she could exorcise the evil spirits which supposedly were tormenting them. No one knows whether all of the seizures were false or some of them real, how much sprang from genuine hysterical illness and how much from self-dramatizing in a feverish desire to attract attention. Some of the actions of the girls may have come from mere high spirits and frivolousness—but some from malevolence, for they were capable of it.

The girls began to show all the classic symptoms of being bewitched. They were pinched and pulled about by invisible hands. They screamed. They went into fits. They writhed in torment. No one else could see the witches and the devils, but the girls could see them clearly. They described the men and women who were torturing them. They told of attacks and enticements. They accused everyone they disliked of being witches. Twelve-year-old Anne Putnam and her mother accused not only Tibuta, but also two aged and respected women of Salem Village, Martha Corey and Rebecca Nurse.

The contagion spread. People tried to outdo each other in being bewitched. Neighbors grasped at a heaven-sent opportunity to even old scores by accusing neighbors of Devil-inspired evil against them. Servants turned on their masters and mistresses. Bewildered small children screamed out against their mothers.

It was wonderful excitement after a long and dreary winter. It caught the imagination and made life worth living. It put New Salem on the map. It was also as devastating as another epidemic of measles or smallpox. The Devil was loose in Massachusetts Bay and bid fair to take over all New England. The situation was out of hand and impossible to ignore. The church was in duty bound to combat a dark and frightening threat; the government was responsible for controlling the outbreak and searching out and punishing the witches who had broken loose to torment the innocent.

Governor Phips appointed a special court of oyer and terminer with Deputy Governor William Stoughton presiding. Among those on the court were Colonel John Hathorne (ancestor of Nathaniel Hawthorne) and Samuel Sewall of the governor's council. His brother, Stephen Sewall, was clerk of the court. The judges, most of them experienced and of high repute, sat in judgment in Salem in July and August 1692 over the accused who were hauled before them. The judges were not bound to accept the verdicts of the jury. The accused were allowed no counsel.

Their accusers vied in exhibition of their sufferings. They were contorted and convulsed. Unseen hands plunged pins into their flesh. They were scalded until blisters were raised. One woman complained that a spectre ran at her with a sharp needle; another was pursued by a spectre in a sheet. The invisible spirits stole their money, forced burning rags into their mouths, and heated branding irons to sear their flesh. None but the plaintiffs, of course, saw, felt, or smelled any of these things.

The Reverend Samuel Parris, the Putnam family of Salem Village, and the Reverend Nicholas Noyes of Salem were unsparing in their efforts to root out suspects and have them brought to trial. Others aided enthusiastically in the witch hunt. Accusations were brought against more than two hundred people. One hundred and fifty suspects were arrested and imprisoned. Either out of panic or the hope that confession would set them free, fifty-five men and women admitted to their guilt as witches. In September 1692 nineteen men and women were hanged on Gallows Hill in Salem, and one man who had refused to testify was pressed to death.

Those hanged were the Reverend George Burroughs of Wells, Maine, who had previously been the minister in Salem Village, Wilmot Reed, Margaret Scott, Susanna Martin, Elizabeth How, Sarah Wildes, Mary Easty, Samuel Wardell, Martha Carrier, Mary Parker, John Proctor, George Jacobs, John Willard, Sarah Good, Rebecca Nurse, Martha Corey, Ann Pudeater, Bridget Bishop, and Alice Parker. Giles Corey was the victim barbarously pressed to death according to English law. Cotton Mather recorded these names which deserve repeating here.

Twenty innocent people were cruelly executed to satisfy the vanity of a group of girls, the credulity and vindictiveness of ignorant people, the conviction of the intellectuals of the time that witchcraft existed, and the stern code of the church and the law. Thomas Hutchinson, its last royal governor, wrote in his *History of the Colony and Province of Massachusetts-Bay*, 1767, "The opinion which prevailed in New England for many years after this tragedy, that there was something preternatural in it, and that it was not all the effect of fraud and imposture, proceeded from the reluctance in human nature to reject errors once imbibed. . . . A little attention must force the conclusion that the whole was a scene of fraud and imposture, begun by young girls, who at first thought of nothing more than being pitied and indulged, and continued by adult persons who were afraid of being accused themselves."

Hutchinson could speak with the judgment and objectivity of three-quarters of a century of perspective and the changed views of another time. These advantages are seldom available to the actual participants in an event. The atmosphere of sadistic orgy, the intoxicating excitement, and the swirling confusion made sane truth more than usually obscure in Salem in 1692.

What is completely untrue is the popular legend—started by malice and propagated by rumor until it became widely held belief—that Increase and Cotton Mather were the instigators of the Salem trials, bloodthirsty persecutors of the innocent, and that Cotton Mather worked to keep the witchcraft scare alive.

Four

I N 1 6 8 4 , four years before his departure for England, Increase Mather published an important book. His *Essay for the Recording of Illustrious Providences* covered unusual storms at sea, magnetism, and earthquakes. In a way he anticipated Benjamin Franklin and his famous experiment seventy years later. Increase Mather wrote that lightning was an irresistible force and noted both that it was faster than the sound of thunder and that, while it left wax unmelted, it fused metals.

In this same book—published eight years before the outbreak in Salem Village and the 1692 trials—Increase Mather said that many things which had been looked upon as proceeding from witchcraft stemmed from other causes. He warned ". . . many innocent persons have been put to death under the notions of witchcraft, whereby much innocent blood hath been shed." As Thomas J. Holmes has pointed out, if Increase Mather's work and warning had been heeded, the Salem witch trials would never have taken place.

Increase Mather was out of the country when the tumult in New Salem started, but Cotton Mather was already involved. He had already dealt with cases of what he and his fellows considered witchcraft and attempted to drive the Devil out of the afflicted bewitched by prayer and fasting. He agreed completely with his father that innocent people could be victimized and he warned early against acceptance of what was called "spectral evidence." This was the unsubstantiated testimony of the accusers. There was no way of knowing whether they lied or told the truth. Spectral evidence had another aspect. It was held at the time that witches were inhabited by familiar spirits, thus were under the spell of the Devil within them. Increase Mather, Cotton Mather, and other important ministers stated their belief that in this way the Devil could use persons who in themselves were innocent, though he appeared in their guise.

In his diary in 1692 Cotton Mather wrote: "For my own part, I was alwayes afraid of proceeding to convict and condemn any Person, as a *Confederate* with afflicting Daemons, upon so feeble an evidence as a *spectral Representation*. Accordingly, I ever testified against it, both publickly and *privately;* and in my *Letters* to the *Judges,* besought them that they would by no means admit itt; and when a considerable *Assembly of Min-*

isters gave in their *Advice* about that Matter, I not only concurred with their *Advice,* but it was *I* who drew it up."

At the request of Sir William Phips, Cotton Mather drew up this document which he and other important Boston ministers signed. It began with these words:

We judge, that in the Persecutions of these and all such Witchcrafts, there is need of a very Critical and Exquisite Caution; Lest by too much Credulity for this received only upon the Devil's Authority there be a door opened for a long train of miserable consequences. . . .

Cotton Mather and his fellows urged that all the judicial proceedings be managed with great care, especially when the defendants were individuals of previously unblemished reputation. They asked the avoidance of noise, crowds, and undue publicity. Cotton Mather demanded that no tests be used which could in any way be suspected of being illegal or unworthy.

Three days before the first witch, Bridget Bishop, was sentenced, Cotton Mather wrote one of the judges, John Richards, "Do not place more stress upon pure Spectre evidence than it will bear. . . . It is very certain that the divvils have sometimes represented the shapes of persons not only innocent, but also very vertuous."

Mather went beyond words to action. He felt the death penalty too severe and that an attempt to cure —certainly an enlightened idea at that time—was preferable to condemnation and irremediable punishment. He suggested that the accused witches be scattered instead of concentrated. He offered to take any six of the accused into his own home and through prayer and fasting try to dispel the evil spirits by which they were enslaved. His offer was ignored.

Cotton Mather attended none of the trials in Salem. He did attend the execution of the Reverend George Burroughs and unwisely made himself conspicuous. By our standards his actions and his words were inexcusable. By those of his time they were approved.

Witchcraft was real and it was terrible. It was particularly heinous when the witch was a minister of God and used his priesthood as a guise to work for the Devil. This is exactly what George Burroughs was condemned for by a tribunal which had sought the advice of the clergy and even of authorities in other colonies. As Lowell pointed out in 1865, it had acted more humanely than comparable courts in Europe.

The Reverend George Burroughs, a small but athletic man, was a Harvard graduate who had been the minister in Salem Village before he left when the church found fault with him and even had him arrested for debt. He was seized at his home in Wells, Maine, and hauled to Salem to answer the charges brought against him by Anne Putnam (of a family which had denounced him ten years before), Abigail Williams, and other young girls. One of them was Mercy Lewis whom Burroughs and his wife had taken into their home in Salem Village and cared for when she was a child.

The girls screamed and cried out in agony when Burroughs was arraigned before the Salem magistrates. Anne Putnam swore that she had seen him presiding over a great meeting of witches in a pasture. Abigail Williams saw him changed into a gray cat before her very eyes and saw Sarah Good grasp the cat in her arms. The Putnam girl also saw Burroughs' two dead wives. They returned from the grave and showed her their wounds in proof that he had murdered them.

Other frightful things were sworn against the astounded and helpless Burroughs. Though he was small, he was possessed of prodigious—unnatural—strength. He could lift a heavy gun with a barrel of six or seven feet just by inserting his finger in its muzzle. In an effort to stop her gossip he had once made his wife sign a paper swearing that she would divulge none of his secrets. Now, it was implied, the world knew what those awful secrets were! All of the evidence was spectral. The brave girls were convincing. It was enough for the judges.

A huge crowd gathered when with four others the Reverend George Burroughs was brought to Gallows Hill, August 19, 1692. Like all the others, he persisted in declaring his innocence. He recited the Lord's prayer calmly and addressed the crowd. On horseback, Cotton Mather called out upholding the judgment of the court and the justice of the verdict. In his eyes, Burroughs had been found guilty after a fair trial, and the guilt was the worse because he was a member of his own sacred profession. In an attempt to ease that stricture, Mather made it a point in his speech that the Reverend George Burroughs had never been ordained.

Samuel Sewall, one of the Salem judges as well as one of the most respected men in Massachusetts Bay—he would become a justice of the Superior Court that very year—was also present. In his famous diary he recorded that a great number of spectators were present at the quintuple hanging, that Mr. Cotton Mather was there, and that the witches all died by a righteous sentence. "Mr. Burroughs by his Speech, Prayer, protestation of his Innocence, did much to move unthinking persons, which occasions their speaking hardly concerning his being executed."

Instead of trying to keep the witch scare with its frightful consequences alive, the Mathers, both father and son, effectively put an end to it.

After establishing the special court in Salem, Sir William Phips had gone off to fight hostile Indians in Maine. He returned to Boston in October 1692 to find that his wife, who had assisted one of the accused to escape, was being accused of being a witch. The Reverend Samuel Willard, pastor of the South Church, and the wife of the Reverend John Hale of Beverly, a Mather relative, had been accused. Phips was at a loss how to deal with the wide-spreading contagion. Increase Mather showed him what to do.

The elder Mather wrote *Cases of Conscience Concerning Witchcraft, Evil Spirits,* etc. In it he repeated the advice which his son had earlier given the court. He held that witches existed and that the Salem judges had done their duty as they saw it—but he said that the Devil could not appear in the person of an innocent and pious man. He denounced superstitious witch tests. He held that the only safe convictions were on the free and open confession of the accused and the sworn statements of two credible persons that they had witnessed the accused doing such things as only the Devil could have prompted. Courageously, Increase Mather wrote:

It were better that ten suspected witches should escape, than that one innocent Person should be condemned. . . . It is better that a Guilty Person should be absolved, than he should be without sufficient ground of Conviction condemned. I had rather judge a Witch to be an honest woman, than judge an honest woman to be a Witch.

Increase Mather had fourteen other leading ministers approve his book and then presented it to the royal governor before its publication. Phips thereupon stopped the proceedings of the special court of oyer and terminer. Fifty accused witches were awaiting trial.

Five others were in prison under sentence of death. Sir William freed them all. He not only terminated the special court, but also ordered judges to cease recognizing spectral evidence. He had other witch cases tried in Superior Court under the system Increase Mather had laid down.

Here, though some of those on the bench had sat in the Salem court, cases were given short shrift. As Cotton Mather reported in his life of Phips, the court, like everyone else, found it impossible to discover the whole meaning of "the things that had happened, and that so many *unsearchable cheats* were interwoven into the *Conclusion* of a Mysterious Business, which perhaps had not crept thereinto at the Beginning of it, they *cleared* the *accused* as fast as they tried them. . . ."

Graves had actually been dug for the five convicted as witches at Salem and for three more condemned in Boston. All were reprieved.

Sir William Phips reported the situation and his decision to the authorities in England, crediting Increase Mather and even using Mather's words to explain his course of action. Though there were witch trials and convictions in other countries for many years, there were never any more in New England.

As Kenneth Ballard Murdock says in the introduction to his *Selections from Cotton Mather*, the myth of Cotton Mather's bloodthirstiness vanishes before the facts.

After the abrupt cessation of the trials he scrupulously avoided any speech or action which might lead to a continuance or reawakening of the hysteria. Instead, as both minister and physician, and far more humanely than most of his contemporaries, he resorted to the gentler methods he had always advocated and had used as early as 1688.

At that time John Goodwin, a mason of Boston, had appealed to him for help with his children. They had been healthy and normal. Suddenly they seemed bewitched and suffered such torments that Dr. Thomas Oakes concluded that nothing but witchcraft could account for their sufferings. Mather took the oldest of the four afflicted children, a girl, into his home and prayed and fasted with her in a quiet house where her diet was regulated and she was carefully tended. Her condition improved, then she relapsed several times. The same happened with the smaller children. It took weeks of devoted care by Mather, his family, and kindly neighbors, but all four children were finally restored to normal health and spirits.

In 1692 Mather's congregation raised more than sixty-two pounds to redeem Mercy Short who had been captured from her home in Berwick, Maine, by Indians who butchered others of her family. Supposedly she had been bewitched by Sarah Good. She was placed in Cotton Mather's care, and the minister and devoted parishioners prayed with the disturbed girl in her room every night for almost a month. Her diet was watched, and she was kept in an atmosphere of rest and quiet. Though left weak in body, she was cured of the Devil —brought back to calm—in March of 1693.

Margaret Rule, a seventeen-year-old girl who exhibited all of the symptoms of being bewitched was then placed in Mather's care and accorded the same treatment of rest and prayer. It has been suggested that she was an imposter who, from whatever impulses of girlish exhibitionism or deliberate fraud, feigned her condition. It is just as possible that, as she claimed, she had suffered unhappy experiences and had convinced herself that she was bewitched. As Abijah Marvin wrote in his life of Cotton Mather, something was the matter with her at any rate. "She was either morally or physically 'out of order.' " Cotton Mather believed that with Margaret Rule he effected another cure.

Mather, John Higginson, William Stoughton, Stephen Sewall, all met with the level-headed Samuel Sewall at his home in Boston, September 22, 1692. They spoke then of writing and publishing a report of the Salem trials. This seems to have been the origin of one of Cotton Mather's best-known and, for him, most unfortunate books. Often quoted in anthologies as evidence of his credulity, it has served mostly to tie his name permanently and unpleasantly with the story he recounted. The book appeared as an official document, the title page of a third edition reading: *The Wonders of the Invisible World; being an account of the Tryals of Several Witches lately executed in New England and of several remarkable curiosities therein occurring.* . . . Published by the special command of His Excellency the Governor of the Province of Massachusetts Bay in New England. Printed first at Boston, in New England; and reprinted at London for John Dunton, at the Raven in the Poultry, 1693.

In *Wonders of the Invisible World* Cotton Mather praised the Salem judges for their attention to duty, described the trials with what seems to later generations too credulous an acceptance of the purported evidence, but once again, condemned convictions based on spectral evidence. The book stood as what seemed a fair statement of the case for the government and the church. Increase Mather read and approved it before its publication. Ministers, magistrates, and most of the general public accepted the book for what it was, but not all.

One who did not like the book and particularly disliked its author was Robert Calef, a cloth merchant who had settled in Boston in 1688. Little is known about him, and there is no record of his having protested against the Salem trials and convictions when the actions took place. It was after they were all over and, largely at the instigation of the Mathers, all suspects had been freed that he attacked the prosecution and viciously attacked the Mathers. Beginning in 1693 he addressed a series of letters to Cotton Mather accusing father and son of trying to foment another witch panic in Boston and, by insinuation, attempted character assassination.

Somehow Calef had obtained Cotton Mather's manuscript account of the case of Margaret Rule. No one knows how he got it or from whom. In his own words, "I received it of a gentleman, who had it of the author, and communicated it to use, with his express consent. . . ." The statement is, of course, ambiguous, as were most of Calef's statements. Without Mather's knowledge or consent, Calef published this account together with his letters to Cotton Mather in *More Wonders of the Invisible World.* The book was finished in 1697 but not published until 1700, when it was printed in London. Some accounts say that no Boston bookseller would issue it.

Calef did not deny the existence of witches. Like everyone else then, he devoutly believed in them. He did deny the justice of the Salem trials and the validity of the evidence. Sensibly he asked of just what witchcraft consisted and how anyone could know with certainty that someone accused was really a witch. Appearing as it did eight years after the event, Calef's book was a deliberate raking up of dead ashes, yet even those who discredit his motives believe it was of value in laying superstition.

In other directions it is impossible to give Robert Calef and his book good marks. Obviously motivated by malice, envy, and, as his intended victims claimed,

political enmity, *More Wonders* was a deliberate on-
slaught on Increase and particularly Cotton Mather.
They were too powerful in state as well as in church
affairs, and the opposing political and religious factions
did not like it. Calef not only called the Mathers bigoted
and superstitious, but also insinuated that they had been
pruriently improper in their examination and treatment
of Margaret Rule.

A long postscript to his book gives further clear intent
of the purpose of Calef's effort. Cotton Mather published his colorful *Life of Sir William Phips* anon-
ymously in London in 1697. Though this had nothing to
do with the purported subject of his book, Calef wrote,
". . . which book, though it bears not the author's
name, yet the style, manner, and matter are such, that,
were there no other demonstration or token to know him
by, it were no witchcraft to determine that the said
mr. Cotton Mather is the author of it. But that he . . .
should step aside into a remote country to put on in-
visibility, though the reason of this be not so manifest,
yet it may be thought to be to gratify some peculiar
fancies. And why may not this be one, that he might
with the better grace extol the actions of mr. Increase
Mather, as agent in England, or as president of Harvard
college, not forgetting his own."

Disdaining controversy of this kind and unwilling to
keep the subject alive, Cotton Mather replied to none
of Calef's letters. He contented himself with writing

in his diary, "There is a sort of Sadducee in this town, a man who makes little conscience of lying, and one whom no reason will divert from his malicious purpose. . . ." Mather did not retort, but he was driven finally to bring suit against Calef for the worst of his insinuations. After Calef made an apology of sorts, he dropped the suit. When *More Wonders* was published the congregation of the Second Church attacked it as calumny in an indignant pamphlet, and Increase Mather had a copy of the book burned in the Harvard Yard.

After careful examination of Calef's book, Abijah Marvin decided that it completely misrepresented the Mathers and that it was "the production of either a very careless, or else a malicious and dishonest man." The comment seems justified, but Calef's book created a sensation when it appeared in Boston, and some of its effect has lasted. It is always pleasanter to believe than to disbelieve scandal, especially when it is circulated about the well known and highly respected. After relapsing exhausted from one of its periodic orgies and beginning to repent, the community always needs a scapegoat. Calef pointed out the availability of the brilliant, influential, and envied Cotton Mather for the post, and many people were glad to accept him as the villain in the Salem piece. I didn't do it—he did! is always welcome relief from the sense of guilt.

Cotton Mather had no hand in causing the Salem scare and the trials. He protested against the methods used by the courts and countered with offers of psychological treatment which he actually used. With his father he was instrumental in bringing the witch persecutions to a sharp close. Yet the myth of his responsibility for the cruel purge started by a group of irresponsible girls in grim Salem Village as it was promulgated by Robert Calef has been happily accepted even by those who should know better.

Always self-confident and often wrong, James Russell Lowell wrote in a long review of the Salem trials in "New England Two Centuries Ago," that ". . . it was the foolish breath of Cotton Mather and others of the clergy that blew the dying embers of this ghastly superstition into flame. . . ." Such uninformed pronouncements have affected people's judgment into the twentieth century. The literary historian, Professor Vernon Louis Parrington, writing in 1917, ridiculed Cotton Mather as righteous and self-centered and said that "the insularity of his thought and judgment grew into a disease." After the fashion of his time, Professor Herbert Wallace Schneider of Columbia, who was something of a popular writer as well as a historian of philosophic thought, dismissed both Increase and Cotton Mather in *The Puritan Mind*, 1930, as "persecuted persecutors" and "pompous incarnations of political theocracy."

Fortunately, Cotton Mather has had more discerning critics. Nathaniel Hawthorne, who was haunted all his life by knowledge of the leading part his great-great-grandfather had played as a judge in the Salem trials, knew the historical writings of Cotton Mather well and used them in many of his stories. Hawthorne was no admirer of the stern and darker aspects of Puritan life and shuddered at the witch trials, but he portrayed Cotton Mather sympathetically more than once.

Henry Wadsworth Longfellow defended Cotton Mather and presented him as he really appeared at the time of the witch trials favorably—and accurately—in "Giles Corey of Salem Farms," one of his *New England Tragedies*.

In a dialogue, Judge John Hathorne is asking for clerical guidance. In giving it, Cotton Mather several times warns the stern judge.

> If God permits
> These evil spirits from the unseen regions
> To visit us with surprising informations
> We must inquire what cause there is for this,
> But not receive the testimony borne
> By spectres as conclusive proof of guilt
> In the accused.

Again, Cotton Mather says,

> Be careful. Carry the knife with such exactness,
> That on one side no innocent blood be shed
> By too excessive zeal, and on the other
> No shelter be given to any work of darkness. . . .

God give us wisdom
In the directing of this thorny business,
And guide us, lest New England should become
of an unsavoury and sulphurous odor
In the opinion of the world abroad!

Mather comforts one of the supposedly bewitched girls by telling her that only through prayer and fasting can the unclean spirits be driven from her. Then he says,

An old man
Gives you his blessing. God be
with you, Mary!

Longfellow made a slight error here. The "old man" was exactly twenty-nine years old at the time. Though he was already famed as a preacher, scholar, and writer, Cotton Mather had hardly started on the major accomplishments which mark his packed career.

Five

COTTON MATHER was a complex individual. He was highly sensitive, intense, determined, proud, incessantly curious, incessantly active, almost incredibly industrious.

Without dispute, he was the most learned man of his time. He read everything and wrote about most of what he read. He was continually adding to the large library which was his delight, and those books which he did not purchase he borrowed. One of his contemporaries said that it seemed as if no book could slip into Boston without Cotton Mather's knowing it, somehow getting hold of it and reading it. In his *Grandfather's Chair* Nathaniel Hawthorne describes Cotton Mather's study as crowded, piled, and heaped with books in English, Latin, Greek, Hebrew, and many other languages— Cotton Mather could read, write, and speak seven of them. The table in the center of the room was strewn with books and manuscripts of sermons, histories, and

religious or political pamphlets in Mather's hand. Hawthorne was using his imagination, but he was probably
not far from the truth.

Cotton Mather was always reading and he was always
writing. Before he was through he would write more
books than any other man in America has ever written
and more than many have read. Beginning with a sermon
preached to the artillery company of Middlesex in 1686
and ending with six titles in 1727, Mather's son Samuel
listed 383. Thomas J. Holmes counted 444. Kenneth
Murdock says more than 450. Grandfather told the
children who listened to him in Hawthorne's tale that
Cotton Mather was a prodigious bookworm, "sometimes devouring a great book, and sometimes scribbling
one as big."

Over the door of his study Mather had painted two
words: BE SHORT. Time was too precious to be
wasted. Visitors could state their business, then go.
Cotton Mather did not heed his own stricture. He was
unfailingly courteous to those who called, unsparing
in his efforts to help all who needed help, instructive but
entertaining in his talk.

Like his father and his clerical grandfathers before
him, he lived his real life in his study. He valued his
library above all his earthly possessions and reveled in
the thought and learning of the world. His appetite for
knowledge was omnivorous, and what he read he used
in his own thinking and writing.

Cotton Mather was as unremitting in his piety as in his reading and writing. His life was one of almost continual prayer. He kept fasts and night-long vigils beyond number, so many, his son Samuel wrote, that he could not list them, for his father kept no count of what was a regular part of his life. Among men Cotton Mather could seem arrogant—he sometimes was—but he was humble before God.

He was introspective. He searched his own mind and heart as sharply and as anxiously as he searched his books. He assigned special significances and duties to even the small habitual actions of his life. When he tended his fire, he thought of improving his life. Paring his fingernails was an occasion for making up his mind to cut all "naughtiness" from his life. The fragrance of tea as he drank a cup was an invitation to fragrant and grateful reflections. He made it a point to think about particular subjects as he wound his watch.

He could not even waste the time while he was dressing, and he outlined a schedule of things to consider as he dressed for every day in the week. On Sunday he commented to himself on himself as pastor; on Monday he looked at himself as husband and father; on Tuesday he thought of a long list of relatives and about what he could do for them; on Wednesday he thought about the Christian Church throughout the world and what further effort he could make on its behalf; on Thursday he thought about the many religious societies to which he could belong and how he could improve their activities; on Friday he planned his continual work with the poor and ill; on Saturday he devoted the time to his own spiritual interests.

William Shakespeare found

> . . . tongues in trees, books in the running brooks,
> Sermons in stones and good in every thing.

Cotton Mather did the same, but he did it in terms of Calvinistic Puritanism. He found signs and portents, indications of God's will or his displeasure everywhere he looked. He found texts for sermons everywhere about him. Any Puritan had only to open his Bible at random to find guidance. Cotton Mather looked into his Bible and into the book of his life. He had only to look down the street or cross his threshold to find moral significances. He could carry this habit to the point of ridiculousness. One day, as he says, he was emptying "the Cistern of Nature" at a wall when a dog trotted along, lifted his hind leg, and did the same thing. This reminded Cotton Mather of the lowly state of man, who was thus akin to a dog.

Despite the staggering number of his published works, some of Cotton Mather's longest books have never been published. Longest of them all, his diary, still incomplete, was not printed until 1911 and 1912. As republished in two large volumes it contains 1,422 large-size pages.

The diary defies description. Though he sought publication for almost everything else he wrote, Mather probably did not intend it for this enormous mass of confession, ejaculation, introspection, praise of God, confusion to his enemies, and what else. He had to have the relief of putting it all down in often touching but sometimes naked and painful revelation. The so-called "stream of consciousness" technique was not invented until the early twentieth century, but Cotton Mather almost used it in the seventeenth and eighteenth centuries. The result is a chaos of piety, ambition, mysticism, pedantry, heartfelt emotion, and miscellaneous memoranda. One biblical warning, Job 31:35, Cotton Mather never heeded: "Oh, that mine adversary had written a book."

Most men and women, including his unfriendly critics, would look as confused and sometimes as silly, if like Cotton Mather they tried to write their lives down in this way. The content would differ, but the revelation of anyone's innermost thoughts, his yearnings, ambitions, and attitudes usually makes him anywhere from ridiculous to repugnant. Fortunately for most people, they do not suffer the compulsions that forced Cotton Mather into such attempted self-realization and consequent self-betrayal. Again, he was not a cautious man or even a temperate one. He had a hot temper as well as a contrite spirit.

All of this pictures Cotton Mather as living for himself and his salvation. That was but one aspect of his character. He was egocentric, but he was not selfish; and he was as active as he was contemplative.

He was often unwell. His feverish industry, his fasts and vigils, saw to that. He suffered headaches, stomach-aches, heartburn, faintness, dizziness at times. When he could, he ignored these discomforts and pushed on in spite of them. He even used them as stimulants. In the midst of the witchcraft holocaust he wrote in his diary, "My *Health* has been lamentably broken for diverse Years, partly by my excessive Toyle, in the public and private Exercises of my Calling, but cheefly, I fear, by my Sins against the *God of my Health;* whence Tis that I have been put many Times to preach, when I had fitter to have been in my Bed, and, when that by Sickness I have been almost utterly disabled for all preparatory Study, yett I have delivered long and hard Sermons, with great Assistance to great Congregations, and come easier out of the Pulpit, than I went into it."

Mather had the modern idea that he should take better care of his body. He also had the vitality which enabled him rise to an occasion, and he was always invigorated by an audience.

He was courageous too. In July 1693 a British fleet brought some 2,000 soldiers from the West Indies into Boston harbor on their way to attack French-held Quebec. They brought with them an epidemic fever which killed many of them and spread through Boston.

Though he knew medicine and thus the danger, Cotton Mather insisted on going to preach to the soldiers and render what aid he could. Aboard the governor's barge on his way to the ships he was taken so violently ill that his friends would not let him proceed. Mather felt that God had saved him "in this *rash undertaking* to go and *pray* and *preach,* among an *herd,* that were so infectious, in probability it would have cost mee my Life; as it proved *mortal* unto others that spent their time among them. . . ."

There were other miracles that year. Cotton Mather recounted them just as he pledged again and again that he would strive to be a shining example to God's people, implored God's help when he undertook new books, and resolved to aid this needy man or woman. Late in 1693 he went to Salem to preach, taking with him three sermons that he planned to preach and then to publish. "The *Notes,* were before the Sabbath, *stolen* from mee, with such Circumstances, that I am somewhat satisfied, the Spectres, or Agents in the *invisible World,* were the robbers." Fortunately he remembered most of what he had written and preached successfully anyway. "So that the Divel gott nothing!"

The marvel was that, while still possessed, Margaret Rule asked whether he had missed his notes. She said spectres had bragged to her that they had stolen them, but she promised he would have them again. Two months after they had disappeared, Mather's notes were found scattered about the streets of Lynn. One wonders what Margaret Rule had actually known about the lost sermons.

Again and again Cotton Mather found proof that his prayers were answered, and as early as May 1681 he recorded an example of the truth of prophecy. "There was an honest Man in the Town whom I lovingly and frequently rebuked, for his neglecting to join himself unto some Church of the Lord Jesus Christ. His indisposition thereunto continuing, I told him, *Well, the God of Heaven hath by his Word been calling upon you; expect now to have Him speak unto you by a Blow!* A few days after this, the honest Man fell down from the top of an House and received a *Blow*, whereof hee lay, for some weeks, as dead. But, coming to himself, one of the first things he thought on, was what I had said unto him; under the sense whereof, hee quickly went and joined himself unto the South church." This kind of interpretation of events was not at all peculiar to Cotton Mather. It was the way religious men and women, the highly educated and intelligent as well as more ordinary people, thought at this time. Yet Mather could carry his cause and effect interpretations to some length sometimes.

In the spring of 1696 he was uncomfortable for two weeks with heartburn, and no medicines he tried provided any relief. In fainting pain, he remembered that Christ has also suffered much the same complaint. He

prayed that for the sake of the horrible heartburn suffered by Christ he be delivered of his lesser pain. "Immediately, it was darted into my Mind, that I had *Sir
Philip Paris's* Plaister in my house, which was good for
the inflammations; and laying this *Plaister* on, I was
cured of my malady."

Once, tragically, it was his failure to pray which
brought on a terrible consequence. Always he prayed
for his children by name. Once, when there were only
three children, he somehow forgot to mention his Me-
hitabel. He had hardly finished his prayers when he
learned that the little girl had been dead for an hour.
Mather felt that he was to blame.

Mather gave both his spiritual and financial help gen-
erously always. He was concerned for condemned criminals and prayed with them. Through his writing he
attempted to ease the plight of Christians caught and
enslaved by the Turks and the Puritans who were persecuted in France. Yet he could break out of his piety
and his philanthropies sometimes to preen himself. In
1699 he listed again the many singular "Favours of
Heaven" especially granted him.

First, that, I should bee such an horribly guilty and filthy
Sinner (in some Respects above any that I know of my
Generation); and that yett my Sin be covered, and I bee
after all my Sin, employ'd in more than ordinary Service,
for the Churches of my Lord Jesus Christ.

Secondly, that I should be a great *Stammerer*, and yet be not only a Preacher of the Gospel, but also my Utterance in my preaching bee not the least *Ornament* of it, and I bee used in speaking more than any man of my Age in the Land, on the most important occasions.

Thirdly, that I should bee a more silly and shallow Person, than most in this Countrey; and yett write and print more Books, and have greater Opportunities to do good by my published Composures, than any Man that ever was in this Countrey, or indeed in all *America*.

The egoism is unashamed in this private writing to himself. Perhaps Cotton Mather needed it to balance his excessive humility. There is also factual truth in what he wrote. He did preach to huge congregations. He did preach on important occasions. Certainly he wrote more books than any other man of his time or ours.

Cotton Mather lived to the full extent of his capacities. He studied, preached, wrote, went about doing good, and used the press consciously as an ecclesiastical and political weapon. He knew the "power of the press" long before that advertising phrase was invented. He went about his Master's business and making enemies. He never shirked from doing the second, and he did not treat his enemies, even powerful ones, lightly or show them either inordinate affection or undeserved forgiveness. In this same month of 1699 he wrote, "A few months ago, the bloody Bishop of *London* (as I

am credibly informed) wrote over to one of his Curates
in this Town, desiring information from him, of whatever treasonable or seditious Passages (I suppose against,
the Church!) I might be charged withal. Doubtless this
little Composure, A letter of Advice to the Churches
of the Non-conformists, if it comes to be published, will
set some edge upon his bloody Inclinations, but the
Lord whom I serve, even the *Great Bishop* of Souls,
will preserve me."

Six

BY THE last decade of the seventeenth century Boston was a busy seaport dealing with the world. The long wharves jutting into the harbor were piled with sugar, spices, tea, casks of wine, and barrels of rum distilled from West Indies sugar. Fish and lumber were the principal exports. Fine furniture, manufactured goods, silver, books—the luxuries as well as the necessities—were the imports.

Boston's aristocratic and wealthy ruling class had its fine homes, its servants and slaves, even its splendid coaches. There was also a large and substantial class of sound mechanics and workmen. A thriving English town as well as the capital of New England, Boston had its dignitaries and its ne'er-do-wells, its destitute, its riffraff and rowdies as well as its respectable and devout. It had well-built homes, well-patronized taverns, shipyards, chandleries, houses of deservedly ill repute, and just across the Charles River, its Harvard.

Wars, politics, and commerce had eroded the idea of unblemished piety held by the Puritan fathers. People were daily becoming more interested in this life than in the next. The Mathers saw this, resented it, preached against it, and were determined to reverse the trend of the times—usually a difficult task and generally not too successful. Stubbornly, Massachusetts Bay pushed headlong toward the democracy which John Cotton had detested.

The province owed its political existence under the 1691 charter to Increase Mather. It was saddled with a royal governor and his entourage but retained most of its freedoms and all of its spirit of independence. Sir William Phips owed his governorship to Increase Mather and his salvation to Cotton Mather. The ship's carpenter transformed into a knight and a powerful official of the crown looked up to his pastor and teacher and did what he could for his benefactors who were the unquestioned heads of the Congregational, i.e., the Puritan, Church.

He favored taxing everyone for the support of the Congregational Church, but too many people of other persuasions had infiltrated Boston. They objected to helping keep churches they did not attend and pointed to the liberty of conscience provision which Increase Mather had had written into the new charter to support their position.

The Mathers were as concerned for Harvard as for

their church. It had been founded almost as part of that church, a training school for Puritan ministers which was taught by a strictly orthodox faculty and governed by orthodox authorities. Gradually Harvard was becoming less rigid, more liberal in its views and in its teaching; a change which alarmed the conservative. The Mathers tried to get a law passed under which only those who espoused the Puritan Church as it had been founded in Massachusetts by their forefathers could becomes Fellows or President of Harvard. Other important ministers worked with them to this end. A provision was inserted in a legislative bill to this end, but it was later removed.

The Mathers could exert considerable control over their governor in some directions, but not in others. Phips was headstrong and determined. As royal governor he was sworn to uphold and enforce the Navigation Acts which forbade importation of goods into the colonies except in English ships manned by English crews and which placed other restrictions on sea commerce. Phips was a freetrader, almost a freebooter, and contemptuous of any hindrances to New England seafaring. He flouted the Acts he was supposed to enforce. An aristocrat by royal favor and a gentleman by virtue of his office, the rough sea captain preferred the society of sailors and shipwrights to that of those who were now, by definition, his peers. He resented any authority other than his own. He outwitted British customs offi-

cials when he could, and when he could not, met them
head-on in angry confrontations. He publicly caned
a captain of the Royal Navy for refusal to obey one of
his orders and dragged the collector of customs around
the dock when that unhappy official attempted to seize
a vessel suspected of illegal trading. Phips got into a
bitter quarrel with Governor Benjamin Fletcher of
New York.

He treated his political opponents cavalierly, packing
the General Court with his adherents and managing to
keep out the opposition. In one way and another he
mismanaged the military affairs of the province, failing
to support a British action against Canada and asking
instead for permission to conduct another campaign of
his own. Energy, probably with pigheaded honesty,
was the Phips hallmark. He lacked any kind of discretion.

Phips finally gave his adversaries plenty of ammuni-
tion to use against him. Their complaints resulted in his
recall to England in 1694 to answer charges of what
amounted to inadequacy in office. He was in London
awaiting trial when he died there, February 18, 1695.

Phips' failure and death were a blow to the Mathers.
Cotton Mather worked now for the appointment of
Joseph Dudley as royal governor of the Province of
Massachusetts Bay. This represented a considerable con-
cession on Cotton Mather's part. Dudley and he had
been avowed adversaries during Dudley's temporary

rule. He had worked against Dudley when he was censor, chief justice, and enforcer of hated laws under Andros. Dudley, who had later spent some time in England and held other crown appointments, was a convert to the Church of England. Undoubtedly Cotton Mather felt that the son of Thomas Dudley, a Harvard graduate of 1665 who had originally intended to become a Puritan divine himself, might still have retained some of his old loyalties. Mather was wrong. Dudley was ambitious, arbitrary, and enamored of the power and social prestige of his office when he was made royal governor after Phips. For the second time he became one of the most hated men in Massachusetts Bay, and Increase and Cotton Mather hated him as thoroughly as anyone else.

Increase Mather remained the head of the Puritan Church; strong, revered, the last of the absolute ecclesiastical powers. Popular preacher, leading scholar, much a public figure, Cotton Mather was his father's strong ally, but it was becoming more and more obvious, probably even to him, that there was little likelihood of his having a churchly throne to inherit. Cotton Mather looked in other directions. It has been said before that Cotton Mather looked backward in his theology but that, with vision few in his time possessed, he looked steadily forward in other and perhaps more important ways and strove impatiently toward new objectives.

Cotton Mather knew his triumphs, but he suffered

misfortune and tragedy too in the last years of the seventeenth and the first years of the eighteenth century.

When he was seventeen or eighteen years old he had bought a Spanish Indian, and the youth who was just beginning his ministry gave him to his father for a servant.

In about 1683 Sir William Phips gave Cotton Mather another such Indian. As the man liked the sea, Cotton Mather let him go to sea and promised to give him his freedom if he would serve him until the end of 1697. The French seized the ship on which the slave was sailing, so Cotton Mather lost him, but he bore the loss as the will of God. He felt anyway that somehow he would get him back. Early in 1696 an English man-of-war captured the French ship, but its captain, Mather said, was a man of no honor or honesty. He refused to return the Indian and said he planned to make a permanent slave of him. Later, against his will, the English captain was forced to return the captive. "And my Servant being so strangely returned," Mather wrote in his diary, "I sett myself to make him a servant of the Lord."

In August 1697 Mather was prostrate on the floor of his empty church thanking God for his many blessings and for making use of him in that very church. "And I offer'd up my Praises unto the Lord Jesus Christ, for his good *Angels*, and their Ministry; and for *My Angel*, and all the Love and Care, wherewith hee has treated mee; and I concluded with a joyful Assurance, that hee had yett more *good Offices* to do for mee, and that hee would gloriously join with mee, in my serving of our Glorious Lord JESUS CHRIST."

Mather's books were coming out continually both in Boston and in London, where many of them were first printed. He reveled in this accomplishment but wrote, "O my God, Grant mee thy Direction about it; and never suffer mee to write any Thing, whereby the Interests of Truth and peace, may bee damnified."

During an epidemic of colds, Mather was confined to his home for a month with headaches, coughing, and fever. Many people died, and he felt at times that he was near death himself. At his recovery he spoke at the Boston midweek lecture to many who like him had just survived the prevailing illness. So many people clamored for copies of his address that Mather gladly prepared it for the press and gave it to a bookseller for setting and sale. It appeared in 1698 as *Mens Sana in Corpore Sano* —A Healthy Mind in a Healthy Body, a phrase popularized two and more centuries later.

When he went to Ipswich and Salem to preach that fall, Cotton Mather visited the grave of his younger brother, Nathaniel, falling on his knees there to praise the Lord for allowing his dear brother's life to be written, read, and serviceable to others "and for sparing me, a barren Wretch, to survive these many years, upon the Earth, to serve His People, in several Parts of the

World." One hundred and forty years later Nathaniel Hawthorne stood where Cotton Mather had stood before him in the old Charter Street Burying Point, where Governor Simon Bradstreet, the Reverend John Higginson, Colonel John Hathorne, and Richard More, a Mayflower passenger, are also buried. He looked at the grave of Nathaniel Mather under blighted apple trees in a corner of the cemetery. Though it was hard to decipher, he could make out the lettering on the stone. It said that Nathaniel Mather had died "an aged man at nineteen years." Hawthorne said that he felt strangely moved at the sight.

Cotton Mather thanked God when his small daughter Nibby fell into the fire but got no burns on her hands or face. In October 1698 he felt that his own life was providentially saved. The rotten planks of a bridge gave way as he was riding over it, and his horse broke through and sank to his shoulders in the stream. Mather clung to his saddle, and, to the astonishment of spectators, the horse, tearing off a shoe, leaped to the shore with him safely on its back. "How happily do the *Creatures* all serve us, while wee are serving, their and our Lord, the Blessed *Jesus!*"

Another son was born to Cotton Mather. He noted his arrival about three-quarters of an hour past one o'clock in the morning on the Lord's Day, July 9, 1699, "an hearty, lusty, and comely infant." There was death too. At about this time when his midweek lecture fell on the same day as a scheduled hanging, the General Court ordered the lecture to be held in a larger place.

Mather was weak and spent from illness and fatigue, but, as so often, he rose to the challenge. As in England, executions were always well attended in the American colonies. "The greatest Assembly, ever in this Countrey preach'd unto, was now come together; to may be four or five thousand Souls. I could not gett unto the Pulpit, but by climbing over *Pues* and *Heads;* and there the spirit of my dearest Lord came upon mee. I preach'd with more than ordinary Assistance, and enlarged, and uttered the most Awakening Things, for near two Hours together."

He wrote a religious tract for sailors. He composed an Indian primer. He concerned himself with the religious welfare of Christians in Spanish America. He complained of imposters coming to Boston and pretending to be ministers and warned all the churches against the mischief these men wrought. He wrote the Anabaptists urging them to repent of employing one of them. One such imposter was a Sam May (real name Sam Axel) who abandoned his wife and children in England after being detected in misconduct and fled to Boston with another woman.

Both Increase and Cotton Mather were sorely tried in 1700 by the organization of the Brattle Street congregation. John Leverett and William Brattle of Increase Mather's Harvard faculty, Simon Bradstreet, and some others joined in a radical movement to change some of the established ways of the Congregational Church. They wished to do away with the public testimony to saving religious experience as a prerequisite to admission to church membership, a drastic change. They also called Benjamin Colman to be their minister in a fourth and more liberal Congregational church in Boston.

Like Cotton Mather, Colman had studied under Ezekiel Cheever. He had graduated with high honors from Harvard in 1692 and taken his M.A. in 1695. A brilliant man, he was in England when he was called to Brattle Street, and in London he had himself ordained a Presbyterian minister. Such ordination did not make him a Puritan cleric in the eyes of the strict Mathers and their fellow clergymen. Matters became worse when the Brattle Street church issued a manifesto proclaiming its adherence to the Westminster Confession of Faith of the Presbyterian Church but at the same time asked fellowship with the other Boston churches.

Cotton Mather was very unhappy about it. "The people of the new Church in Boston, who by their late Manifesto, so assaulted all the Churches of New England, went on in an ill way, and in a worse Frame, and the Town was filled with Sin, and especially with Slanders (*for grievous Revolts must be managed with Slanders*) wherein especially my Father and myself were sufferers."

People took religious disputes seriously in Boston in 1700. Not only clergymen but entire congregations warred bitterly, for the church and things spiritual were still the most important things in the lives of the devout. The Mathers drew up a protest, which they titled an *Antidote* against the infection from Brattle Street. Then, after the first sheet had been printed, Cotton Mather stopped the press and drew up a proposal. Even in churchly matters he was never inflexible. His compromise was that Brattle Street recognize its covenant with God and with one another, after the early Puritan fashion, and that it acknowledge the communion of Boston churches on the foundation of the agreement of the United Brethren (of Congregational and Presbyterian churches) which Increase Mather had helped bring about in England.

Surprisingly, Brattle Street agreed, and the dispute had a happy ending which awakened Cotton Mather's gratitude. Differences were forgotten as the churchly disputants kept public fast together, and the Mathers appeared in the Brattle Street pulpit. Increase Mather preached to the new congregation on following peace with holiness, and Cotton Mather concluded the service with prayer. Cotton Mather and Benjamin Colman, who became, with him, an active Fellow of Harvard, a clear writer and a man of liberal views for his time, became and remained close friends.

By mid-1702 Cotton Mather's wife had been so ill, seemingly of tuberculosis, for fourteen weeks that her life was despaired of. Nurses were in constant attendance, and Mather did all he could to care for and comfort her. She seemed to improve, but declined again, and soon it was only too clear what the end would be.

As his wife lay dying, his children and a "godly maid" sickened. Eight-year-old Nibby came down with the raging smallpox. Five-year-old Nancy and then three-year-old Increase were stricken. They kept calling for their father, and he prayed with them, he says, not less than ten or a dozen times a day. The large house was full of illness. Even Cotton Mather's study had to be turned into a sickroom.

It has been said that Cotton Mather appears at his worst in his diary. This is inevitable when a man writes so unguarded an account of his inner life. He also appears at his best in the diary. The man who writhed prostrate before his God, flailed at his enemies, and tried to satisfy the craving of his quick and eager mind with copious reading and continual writing is nobly human in the affecting passages that describe this personal tragedy.

"At last, the black Day arrives; Tuesday, the first of December, 1702. I had never yett seen such a black Day in all the Time of my pilgrimage. *The Desire of my Eyes* is this Day to be taken from me. Her death is lingring, and painful. All the forenoon of this Day, she lies in the Pangs of Death, sensible until the last Minute or two before her final Expiration."

Cotton Mather could not remember all that passed between them or what they said. He knew his wife composed and devout, ready to go to God. He asked her to tell him truly what fault she saw in him. She said none and that his words had brought her nearer God. Abigail Phillips Mather was thirty-two years old, and she and Cotton Mather had been married for sixteen years; as the heartbroken man noted, just one-half her life on earth.

When I saw to what a point of Resignation, I was now called of the Lord, I resolved, with His help therein to Glorify Him. So, two Hours before my lovely Consort expired, I kneeled by her Bed-Side, and I took into my two Hands, a dear Hand, the dearest in the World. With her then in my Hands, I solemnly and sincerely, gave her up unto the Lord; and in token of my real RESIGNATION, I gently putt her out of my Hands, and laid away a most lovely Hand, resolving that I would never touch it more!

This was the hardest and perhaps the bravest Action that ever I did. . . . She continued until near two o'clock in the Afternoon. And the last sensible Word that she spoke, was to her weeping Father, *Heaven, Heaven will make amends for all.*

Mather then prayed with the others weeping in the room. He had employed almost one hundred watchers to nurse his wife, so long ill, and his three sick children, all of whom recovered. To each of them he gave one of his published tracts with pasted in it a love poem to his dead wife.

Go then, my Dove, but now no longer *mine;*
Leave *Earth* and now in heavenly Glory shine.
Bright for thy Wisdome, Goodness, Beauty here;
Now *brighter* in a more angelick Sphaere.
Jesus, with whom thy soul did long to bee,
Into his Ark, and Arms, has taken thee. . . .

Seven

IN THIS same year of his wife's death Cotton Mather's most important book was published in London. This was his *Magnalia Christi Americana* (The Mighty Deeds of Christ in America). It was a huge leather-bound folio, its parts numbered separately, of nearly eight hundred pages. Not for one hundred and eighteen years was this work, first printed at the Bible and Three Crowns in Cheapside near the Mercers Chapel, reprinted in this country. Then it was published in a more manageable two volumes which are difficult to come by in libraries now. Almost entirely in capital letters of various sizes with printer's rules separating the parts, the title page of this first American edition reads:

MAGNALIA CHRISTI AMERICANA: or the ECCLE-SIASTICAL HISTORY OF New-England from its first planting in the Year 1620, unto the Year of Our Lord,

1698. In Seven Books. By the Reverend and Learned
COTTON MATHER, D.D.—F.R.S. and Pastor of the
North Church in Boston, New-England. In Two Volumes.
First American Edition, from the London Edition of 1702.
Hartford: Published by Silus Andrus. Roberts & Burr,
Printers, 1820.

The *Magnalia* needed a long title page, for it was a
long and packed book, an impressive, all-inclusive book.
Into it Mather crammed scores of eulogistic biographies,
accounts of miracles, intricate Calvinistic theology, war
reports, the last words of criminals before their executions—and even, as he acknowledged when the book
first appeared in London, errors. In that first folio he
quoted a Roman author to the effect that it is impossible to find "a Book Printed without *Errata's*." He then
listed those he had found even before the book was published, probably sending his corrections from Boston to
the printers in London. Sheets of errata together with
advertisements for other books by the London publisher
lengthened the already long folio.

The *Magnalia* gives all the facts as Mather knew them
or could find them from the settlement of Plymouth by
the Pilgrims to the year in which he sent his manuscript
to London. This, he says in effect, is what happened.
This is what it was like when it happened. These are
the men who led the church and state, what they did
and what they were like.

The *Magnalia Christi Americana* is sound history and unsound gossip. It imposes the Puritan interpretation of life on what it records. Yet it is one of the most valuable books to come out of colonial times and one on which generations of scholars, historians, and imaginative writers have leaned heavily. Cotton Mather spent four years writing it. In July 1693 he determined to write the church history of Massachusetts as a service to God. Fellow ministers to whom he confided his plan encouraged him. He compiled, edited, wrote, and completed most of the work before the end of 1697. A friend, Robert Hackshaw, paid for publication of the huge manuscript.

Volume One contains three of the seven books that comprise the whole of the *Magnalia*. In them are seven chapters of "Antiquities": the lives of the governors and magistrates of Massachusetts Bay; and the lives of sixty "famous divines" of New England. Volume Two contains a history of Harvard; a history of the many acts passed in the various synods of the Congregational Church; eight chapters of "many illustrious, wonderful Providences, both of mercies and judgments on divers persons in New-England"; and six chapters of The Wars of the Lord, "Being an History of the manifold Afflictions and Disturbances of the Churches in New-England, from their various adversaries, and the wonderful methods and mercies of God in their deliverance.—To which is subjoined An Appendix of Remarkable Occurrences which New-England had in the wars with the Indian savages, from the year 1683 to the year 1693."

Much of what we know of William Bradford (Mather calls him "Galeacious Secundus"), the leader of Plymouth, and of John Winthrop ("Nehemias Americanus") is in the *Magnalia*. There are lives of Francis Higginson, Jonathan Burr, Peter Hobart, Henry Dunster, and Peter Bulkeley, who was Ralph Waldo Emerson's first American ancestor and the founder of Concord. There is a life of Richard Mather and a long biography of "The Renowned John Eliot." Mather considered John Cotton, John Norton, John Wilson, John Davenport, and Thomas Hooker so important that he placed them in a chapter by themselves.

Titling it "Pietas in Patriam," Mather included the whole of his *Life of Sir William Phips, Knt.*, "Late Captain General and Gouvernour in Chief of the Province of Massachusetts-Bay, New England," thus acknowledging its already well-known authorship. He followed it with an elegy in verse between heavy black mourning borders. He included a long letter from Increase Mather to Dr. John Leusden, professor of Hebrew in the University of Utrecht, testifying to the success of spreading the Gospel among the Indians.

The *Magnalia* must have appeared an awesome book when it first reached Boston from London. It *is* an awesome book, Cotton Mather's most formidable literary and historical accomplishment. It served its own time, and it has served posterity well.

In a long General Introduction to it Cotton Mather wrote, "Reader! I have done the part of an impartial historian. . . ." From his viewpoint and the Puritan viewpoint, he had done exactly that, but, in this connection, impartiality had not the same meaning to Mather and his readers as it has now. His title indicates just how Cotton Mather viewed his material. In the Bible Commonwealth which hardy men and women founded in the cold wilderness of New England everything that happened happened as it did because God so willed it. As a faithful historian, Cotton Mather had not only to recount events, but also to show how they fitted into God's plan. He had to explain as well as to narrate; to expound as a preacher as well as to record as a historian. His book has thus a double value as factual history and as a revelation of the essential Puritan outlook and attitude. No one—not Sir Walter Raleigh, Edward Gibbon, Thomas Carlyle, or Henry Adams—has ever written an objective history, for that is impossible, and Cotton Mather did not pretend to. He stated his purpose.

It was to write of the wonders of Christianity in America—to relate "the considerable matters" that attended the first settlement of the New England colonies; to "introduce the actors" and then the "notables of the only Protestant University, that ever shone in that hemisphere of the New World." He wrote of the synods which saved the Puritan religion from temptations within and enemies without. Piety as well as accuracy was Cotton Mather's intent, and it was an intent understood and approved by his readers.

The introductions to many books in the twentieth century are often disguised—or undisguised—advertisements. It is amusing to find what amounts to a publisher's blurb in Cotton Mather's introduction to the *Magnalia*.

Let my readers expect all that I have promised them in this bill of fare; and it may be they will find themselves entertained with yet many other passages, above and beyond their expectations, deserving likewise a room in history; in all which there will be nothing but the author's too mean way of preparing so great entertainments to reproach the invitation.

The *Magnalia Christi Americana* should have brought Cotton Mather the one reward he desperately coveted. His church opponents and political adversaries forced Increase Mather to relinquish the Harvard presidency in 1701. The most learned man in New England, its renowned author and its most popular preacher, Cotton Mather wanted intensely to succeed his father. As a Fellow, he had been active in Harvard affairs for years. He was, and knew himself to be, eminently qualified for the post. Two things hindered his appointment: his insistence that Harvard retain the Puritan orthodoxy of its founders and the enmity of Governor Joseph Dudley.

Cotton Mather was actually named president of Harvard by the House of Representatives of the General Court in 1703, but the appointment was overruled. Mather kept trying, and even twenty years later was hopeful of the post and bitter when it was withheld. Though he was told in May 1724 that he would probably be made president of Harvard, he was ignored. In his diary he wrote that "yesterday the six Men who call themselves the Corporation of the College mett, and Contrary to the epidemical Expectation of the Countrey, chose a modest young Man, of whose piety (and little else) every one gives a laudable character." The corporation's choice was the Reverend Joseph Sewall. He declined the honor. Mather told himself that his release from all expectation from Harvard was a mixture of good and bad for him, but he could not forget the slight.

Again in his diary he wrote, "The Corporation of our miserable College do again (upon a fresh Opportunity) treat me with their accustomed Indignity and Malignity." This time Harvard had chosen Mather's friend, the Reverend Benjamin Colman. He too refused, and the job went to Benjamin Wadsworth who took office in July 1725.

Joseph Dudley was no more palatable the second time around than he had been the first. Despite his nativity and upbringing, he considered himself an English gentleman rather than a New England provincial and conducted himself as the haughty official of the powerful English crown. He was continually at odds with the General Court which represented the Massachusetts Bay colonists, contemptuous of its wishes, and arbitrary in his actions.

When the new royal governor called on him in June 1702, Cotton Mather was blunt. He told Dudley he had arrived when people were particularly apprehensive about what he might do. He advised him to align himself with no party. He suggested that he not let it be said that he took advice from his father and him or, on the other hand, from the opposition as represented by John Leverett and his associates. In other words, Mather advised that Dudley keep himself free of factional disputes. Dudley (Mather described him in his diary as "the wretch") immediately told Leverett and Byfield that Cotton Mather had been talking against them.

The differences between the Mathers and Dudley widened, and the animosity grew. When Dudley appointed Leverett president of Harvard in 1707, Cotton Mather's ire and disappointment drove him to recklessness. In a bitter letter, he reminded Dudley that his writing King William on his behalf had been an important influence in his being appointed royal governor. When he was in office, Sir William Phips had been told that the governorship could be worth twelve hundred pounds a year on the side, but Phips had said, not to an honest man. Obviously it was proving worth at least that to its present incumbent.

Cotton Mather flatly accused Joseph Dudley of bribery and corruption. He said that the provincial government was carrying on unlawful trade with England's enemies. He accused the governor of irregularities in both the civil and military affairs of the province. In a complementary letter sent the same day Increase Mather made some of the same charges. Both father and son saw bitterly now that there could be no return to the time when ministers exerted control over civil leaders. This was their renunciation of any attempt to restore the old order. They had their say, sharply and finally, and withdrew from the political arena.

When his wife died, Cotton Mather was a celebrated and admired figure in Boston. He stood high in popular esteem and was well liked by those closest to him. Impatient, hot-tempered, he made enemies—as does any man who takes a stand—and seems to have enjoyed defying them, but he was also a man of charm and presence. Benjamin Colman wrote this of him, "It was *Conversation* and Acquaintance with him, in his familiar and occasional Discourses, and private Communications, that discovered the vast compass of his Knowledge, and the Projections of his Piety; . . . . Here he excell'd;

here he shone; being exceedingly communicative and bringing out of his *Treasury* things new and old, without measure. Here it was seen how his Wit, and Fancy, his Invention, His Quickness of thought, and ready Apprehension were all consecrated to God, as well as his Heart, Will, and Affections. . . ."

Mather talked warmly to visitors, suiting his talk to their capacity. He talked of what he had been reading, one of his devices of remembering it and storing it for future use. He tried to advise those who needed and sought what he could offer. In the pulpit he was matchless in Boston.

Cotton Mather was famous and attractive. He was a prize now which more than one Boston woman was determined to catch. One young woman was particularly forthright. She did not simply lay siege. Confident of victory, she attacked head-on. Two months after the death of Mather's wife she wrote to him. Then she called. A gentlewoman, said to have been beautiful, she told Mather that she was so charmed with him that she was forced to request that he marry her. Knowing her man, she explained that she felt conjugal association with him would make her salvation sure.

Cotton Mather had four young children who needed a mother, but he politely demurred. He admitted that his suitor was a young gentlewoman of such accomplishment that no other compared with her, but this was not what he wanted. The rumor quickly spread that the minister of the Second Church was wooing the girl. Mather was flattered but embarrassed. As the campaign waxed hotter, he felt that it must be a design of Satan to entrap him, ruin his family, and destroy his ministry. Finally he was forced to write a blunt letter to the mother of his persistent follower, making his rejection of their proposal clear. The scorned women threatened dire consequences, but later softened, and mother and daughter became his—more distant—admirers again.

In July 1703, but two houses away, Cotton Mather found a young widow of about thirty, "a Gentlewoman of Piety and Probity and a most unspotted Reputation; a Gentlewoman of good Witt and Sense, and Discretion at ordering a Household; a Gentlewoman of incomparable Sweetness in her Temper, and Humour; a Gentlewoman honourably descended and related; and a very comely person." Daughter of Dr. John Clark, Elizabeth Hubbard had been widowed four years before. She and Cotton Mather were married and eventually had six children, only one of whom survived the father.

In 1710 Cotton Mather received gratifying recognition of his fame abroad. In Scotland, Glasgow University conferred upon him its degree of Doctor of Divinity. With the degree came letters from scholars testifying to the respect in which he was held as a scholar and writer. A ring accompanied this signal honor. On it were engraved a tree, Psalm 1:3 ("And he shall be like a tree planted by the rivers of water"), and "Glascua rigavit." Friends persuaded Cotton Mather that he could wear the ring without vanity. His wearing it would honor the givers and instill piety in those who saw it.

In 1710, too, Cotton Mather published his most popular book. A vigorous small book that went through many editions into the next century, it is still read. It is written in simple, direct, and colloquial language without the literary embellishments of his more pretentious *Magnalia*. Dedicated to Sir William Ashurst, who had been on the council with Increase Mather in England, the book was:

BONIFACIUS, AN ESSAY Upon the GOOD, that is to be DEVISED and DESIGNED BY THOSE Who Desire to Answer the Great END of *Life*, and to DO GOOD While they *LIVE* . . . Boston in *N. England*: Printed by *B. Green*, for *Samuel Gerrish* at his Shop in Corn Hill, 1710.

Generally known as the "Essays to Do Good," Cotton Mather's book made "humble proposals of unexceptional methods" to professional men and to those in civil authority. In a long preface Mather confessed that he had not spent as much time in writing it as Descartes spent in solving one problem in geometry, but that he thought well of his little piece and felt that doing what he proposed would give real and lasting satisfaction to those who heeded his advice. A general chapter on essays to do good was followed by others titles: The Duty to Oneself; Relative to Home and Neighborhood; Ministers; Schoolmasters; Magistrates; Physicians; Rich Men; Officials and Lawyers; Reforming Societies; Desiderata; and Conclusion.

Bonifacius is a practical handbook of altruistic social decency. Mather suggests, naturally, that magistrates seek and heed the advice of ministers. He advises ministers to take particular note of widows, orphans, and the afflicted; that they devote one afternoon a week to pastoral calls—and let people know in advance that they are coming. He urged ministers to read and study.

He asked probity, justice, and mercy of officials and lawyers. John Cotton's father had been a lawyer, he reminded his readers, but when people came demanding that he sue someone for them, he always tried first to effect a reconciliation. "There has been an old complaint, *that a good lawyer seldom is a good neighbor.*" He asked lawyers to refute the truth of this by decent behavior.

Cotton Mather asked schoolmasters to instill piety, to bring up children for the Lord, to reward the diligent —and to keep their hands off their charges. He attacked corporal punishment more than a century before A. Bronson Alcott made its removal from the school part of his educational credo and Henry Thoreau quit his teaching job rather than administer it. Always sympathetic with the young, Mather wrote sharply:

Let it not be said of the scholars, "They are brought up *in the school of Tyrannus.*" Pliny says that *bears* are the fatter for beating. Fitter to have the conduct of *bears* than of ingenuous *boys*, are the masters that can't give a *bit* of learning, but they must give a *knock* with it. . . . The harsh, fierce . . . way of treating the children, too commonly used in the *school* is a dreadful *curse* of God upon our miserable offspring. . . . It is boasted now and then of a *schoolmaster*, that such and such a *brave* man had his education under him. There is nothing said, how many that might have been *brave men*, may have been destroyed by him; how many *brave wits*, have been dispirited, confounded, murdered by his *barbarous* way of managing them.

This is forthright stuff which probably displeased some of the pedagogues who read *Bonifacius*. His own revered Ezekiel Cheever once boasted that he had flogged seven of the judges on the Massachusetts bench when they were boys. Mather's was modern doctrine, psychologically reasoned, and he was never more modern than in his chapter on the home and neighborhood.

In today's jargon, Cotton Mather was "community-minded." He was deeply concerned for his fellows, always for the poor, the ill, the "underprivileged." He urged not only monetary relief for the poor but charity of soul. He suggested that rich men give poor children a liberal education. He urged on men of wealth the duty of public service. Of course, he proposed piety again and again, but Mather was practical, and he knew people. His suggestions were pointed and his language was almost slangy here.

If any *children* in the neighborhood, are under no education, don't allow 'em to continue so. Let care be taken that they be better educated. . . .

If any in the neighborhood, are taking to *bad* courses, lovingly and faithfully admonish them. . . .

You must not think of the *good* you do as a pouring of water into a pump, to draw out something for yourselves. . . .

Do good unto those neighbors who will *speak ill* of you, after you have done it.

Cotton Mather warned against backbiting and vanity in community affairs. What he asked, again and again, was simple human decency.

Cotton Mather was no recluse. He was always up and around and about, and he believed strongly in community action. He favored religious societies and organizations for the suppression of vice and crime and was active in a score of them. Through example as well as precept, he was the social reformer of his day.

Mather had stopped looking back in political and church affairs. He was more concerned now with the present and the future than with the past. He had always acted more liberally than he spoke. Alert and vigorous in his middle years, he was giving more thought to social and scientific interest—and he was always giving of himself and what worldly goods he had.

We have the best possible testimony to the effectiveness of *Bonifacius*. The most practical and perhaps the most intelligent American man of business and state affairs in the eighteenth century acknowledged his lasting debt to Cotton Mather and his "Essays to Do Good."

Mather's first effect on Benjamin Franklin was personal and physical. After Mather's first trip to Philadelphia, the young Franklin returned the visit by calling on Cotton Mather in his study. The two men were still talking as Mather saw his visitor out of the house through a narrow passage. Suddenly he called out, "Stoop! Stoop!" Franklin did not understand until his head crashed against a low overhead beam.

Mather improved the bruising opportunity. "You are a young man," he told Franklin, "and have the world before you; stoop as you go through it, and you will miss many hard thumps." Franklin remembered and said years later, "This advice, thus beat into my head, has frequently been of use to me; and I often think of it, when I see pride mortified, and misfortune brought upon people by their carrying their heads too high."

Cotton Mather's *Bonifacius* did even more for Benjamin Franklin. In 1784, when he was an old man, Franklin wrote Mather's son Samuel, "When I was a boy, I met with a book entitled, 'Essays to Do Good'.

. . . several leaves of it were torn out, but the remainder gave me such a turn of thinking, as to have an influence on my conduct throughout life; . . . and if I have been, as you seem to think, a useful citizen, the public owed all to the advantages of that book."

Eight

COTTON MATHER was nearly murdered in the summer of 1712. A ship's captain decided that the minister had singled him out when he preached against evil conduct. Probably drunk, he descended on Mather's house about nine in the evening with drawn cutlass, swearing that he would cleave Mather in two and roaring that he would be glad to lie a year in hell for the privilege. Neighbors overpowered the raging seadog and carted him away.

Mather rejoiced when he received a legacy of eighty pounds and his family received other gifts. He gave so much of his income to charity that he was often in need of money. This same month he put the child of poor parents to school at his own expense. He was already maintaining a school for Indians. He gave money and advice to one of his schoolmasters of forty years before who was now poor and crippled. Once in 1712 he mixed a little gambling with his charity. He was

putting aside twenty shillings each to help several country ministers, but he could aid only four out of seven,
so he wrote their names on slips of paper and drew
lots to choose the four.

Cotton Mather was tender-hearted and generous in
many ways. When part of his large congregation found
it a hardship to cross part of Boston Bay to attend the
Second Church, he urged them, though it would lessen
his flock, to build a church of their own. He offered
to contribute to its support from his own salary. The
church was built, and he assisted at the installation of
its minister.

With the other Indian commissioners he rode twenty
miles in rain to Natick where there was one of the
villages of "Praying Indians" founded by John Eliot.
He led services there and was well satisfied with the
day—but not with another effort where Indians were
concerned. They had carried off a young kinswoman
in the raid on Deerfield in 1704 and taken her to Canada
where she married an Indian and was converted to
Catholicism. When she made her way back to Boston,
she was unmoved by the prayers of Cotton Mather and
other ministers, refused "redemption," and remained a
Catholic.

The Puritans did not observe Christmas. On Christmas
Day in 1712 Cotton Mather, preaching on "Grace De-
fended," showed that the exact date, even the year, of
Christ's birth is unknown, and he asked a question.

"Can you in your Conscience think that our *Holy Saviour* is honoured by *Mad Mirth*, by Long *Eating*, by hard *Drinking*, by lewd *Gaming*, by rude *Revelling*; by a Mass fit for none but a *Saturn*, or a Bacchus, or the Night of a *Mahometan Ramadan?*"

Often triumph and tragedy seemed to come to Cotton Mather in the same year, and he knew both in 1713.

Increase Mather had always been interested in science, and he wrote as a scientist in his *Essay for the Recording of Illustrious Providences*. In England he had been the friend and associate of scientists. He had formed a scientific society in Boston, and Cotton Mather had heard the science of the day discussed in his own home. In Harvard he had studied science and medicine as well as theology.

The Old World was curious about the natural history of the New. When the eminent minister and geologist of London, Dr. John Woodward, wrote asking Cotton Mather for North American fossils and any information he could supply about them, Cotton Mather responded eagerly. He did far more than Woodward asked. His reports and observations were quickly recognized in London as those of a man of scientific attainments, and in 1713 he was notified that he had been made a Fellow of the Royal Society. No other American minister had ever been elected to this august body, and Cotton Mather was one of the few Americans of any kind elected during the first half of the eighteenth century.

Henry Thoreau once said with his wry humor that he was a great traveler about his village of Concord. Cotton Mather was a great traveler in Boston and Cambridge. This was his bailiwick. He visited surrounding towns and villages but seldom went far, and he seems never to have left New England. Yet he was a man of the learned world of London and Glasgow. His interests encompassed Europe, the English colonies, and South America. He kept up a wide and continuous correspondence with a half hundred men of importance abroad. Ministers, mathematicians, philosophers, scientists, and even the Lord Chancellor of England were among them. For nearly twenty years he kept up a friendly interchange with Dr. Isaac Watts, pastor of the Mark Lane congregation in London and composer of some six hundred hymns, including, "O God, Our Help in Ages Past," "When I Survey the Wondrous Cross," and "Jesus Shall Reign Where'er the Sun."

Once in his diary he wrote despairingly, "My Slothfulness! My Slothfulness!" He may have believed that he was indolent compared to what he wished to be, but there was nothing lazy about Cotton Mather, and his nervous vitality seemed inexhaustible.

He wrote this when he was preaching to huge congregations, promoting reform societies, keeping his fasts and vigils, looking after the physical and spiritual welfare of his family, and escorting condemned men to the gallows. Once it was an Indian of nineteen who had got drunk and murdered his friend. Unlettered, he did not even know, Mather says, that he had a soul. Under the minister's tutelage the bewildered Indian professed belief in Christ and repentance. Again, it was six pirates to whom Mather gave what comfort he could before he conducted them to their execution.

It was customary for young men to accompany a minister on horseback when he rode to outlying towns to preach. Cotton Mather usually took some young man with him when he thus rode abroad so that he could pray with him in private at the inns or lodging where they stayed. He liked the young. He was always delighted with the "little damsels" in his congregation, and he was the friend of boys. Dr. Samuel Mather, when he wrote the story of his father's life, said, "When he went into any considerable towns, he would for the most part beg 'Play-Days' for the Boys; and, as a condition for their being excused from school, he would enjoin some Religious Task upon them."

Many entries in his diary Cotton Mather prefixed with the initial letters "G.D.," meaning "good device." Again and again he resolved to show even greater consideration for his aging father. He noted aged Negroes who needed his help. One "G.D." in October 1713 read: "An Aged Gentlewoman, whose Milk I suck'd when I was an infant, is now in another Town, lying in a poor Clinic under a Palsey, and in indigent circumstances. I must send Releefs unto her." Among the poor and aged whom he noted that he must look after was an eighty-eight-year-old man who had actually fought in Cromwell's army.

Amid all of this the Rev. Mr. Cotton Mather, D.D., F.R.S., as he could now sign himself, found time for his *Curiosa Americana.*

This was the title which he gave collectively to his many reports of scientific phenomena to the Royal Society. From 1712 through 1724 there were about eighty of them on a wide variety of subjects. The contents of some of these "composures" seem quaint now. Mather sometimes mingled superstition with fact, but so did all the learned scientists of the day. Mather was well abreast of the scientific thought of his time and in advance of many of the scientists abroad whom he addressed.

Mather sent these communications first to Dr. Woodward, then to Richard Waller, who was secretary of the Society. He incorporated already published or reported phenomena and occurrences and described others that he had seen with his own sharp eyes. He wrote of the discovery of the teeth and bones of a giant found near Claverack, thirty miles from Albany. He wrote of monstrous births of medical interest, of remarkable recoveries from wounds, of thunder and lightning, of cases of longevity, and of the Indian divisions of time by sleeps, moons, and winters.

He described the vast flocks of pigeons, thousands in

a flock, in Massachusetts Bay, telling of flocks that covered the best part of a mile. One of his neighbors had brought down a dozen with a single shot, and pigeons sold for two or threepence the dozen. Farmers fed them to their hogs. Mather noted that cock pigeons care for the young for part of the day, the hens for the other.

Mather paid particular attention to nature, and, unusual at the time, wrote often of its beauties. He reported that men digging a well in Springfield came on axe-marked trees and chips and butternuts twenty feet below ground level, and he told of a "Triton." Two men going by boat from Milford to Brainford, Connecticut, saw a merman about five or six feet long, with hairy face, arms, shoulders, and breast but the lower body of a fish with forked tail and two fins. He wrote of "A Monster." This was Siamese twins in Boston.

In one report Cotton Mather wrote pleasantly of the muskrat. "We have a little Animal called a *Musquash*, pretty frequently lodging about ye Brooks . . . a small Beast, that lives in Shallow Ponds where it builds notable Houses of Earth and Sticks and feeds upon *Calamus Armomaticus*. It has a strong scent of Musk, especially about ye month of May." Mather told the wondering Europeans of other American animals and birds: the moose, the sea lion, the water-dove, the wild turkey, the eagle. He told of an Indian who handled a rattle-snake without danger by first anointing himself with the fat of the kite, a bird which killed and ate rattle-snakes. He told of the boneless and toothless sharks which people took off Cape Cod for the oil in their livers.

Mather tried to satisfy European curiosity about American flora, particularly about plants with medicinal value and their use in various Indian and colonial remedies. He had the same appetite for marvels as his scientific peers abroad and told of the remains of a dragon, over one hundred and fifty feet in length from head to tail, found near the falls of the James River in Virginia. Exploring nearer home, he wrote of the eclipse observed at Cambridge, September 23, 1717. He gave a graphic description of the great Boston blizzard of February 28, 1717. His reports covered everything from a clinical description of the idiot daughters of a paralyzed man in Dunstable to climatic influences and the strength of the imagination. Often his attitude was very modern. His mind was sharp and his pen a tool he had thoroughly mastered.

At one point Cotton Mather sent Dr. Woodward a box of twenty or thirty fossils which he obtained from John Winthrop, grandson of Connecticut's first governor. Again, he sent some squash seed given him by Samuel Sewall. With them he penned a humorous note. "It comes by a Tame Indian; for so ye Europeans are wont sometimes to denominate ye Children that were born in these Regions."

Some of this work Cotton Mather did under great emotional stress. November 1, 1713, twins were born to his second wife. The girl was named Martha; the boy, Eleazar. Three days later his wife, a maid, and his small daughter Jerusha, came down with measles. The maid and Elizabeth Hubbard Mather, to whom he had been happily married for ten years, died. Then the newborn twins died. Between nine and ten o'clock in the evening on the day of their funeral, "my lovely Jerusha expired. She was Two years, and about Seven Months old . . . Lord, I am oppressed; undertake for me!"

Once more Mather was stricken, and four years later began a new and long-drawn-out unhappiness. There were juvenile delinquents in 1713 too. In his diary in the spring of 1713 Mather had written: "There are Knotts of Riotous Young Men in the Town. On purpose to insult piety, they will come under my Windows in the middle of the night and sing profane and filthy songs. The last night they did so, and fell upon people with clubs taken off my wood-pile. Tis high time, to call in the help of Government . . . for the . . . suppression of these disorders."

Then as now, rowdies had little regard for the sufferings of others or their peace of mind, and Cotton Mather had to cope with one even nearer home. His son Increase, born of his first marriage, was proving an incorrigible deliquent. The boy whom his father had named proudly for his own father and whom fondly he called "Cresy," got into one unsavory scrape after another. "O! My son *Increase,* my Son, my Son!" Mather wrote in his diary. Neither his admonitions nor his prayers with his son in the solitude of his study helped. In 1717 Cresy was accused, evidently with reason, of getting a woman of the town with child. "Oh! Dreadful Case! Oh, Sorrow beyond any that I have mett withal! what shall I do now for the foolish Youth! what for my afflicted and abased Family? My God, look mercifully upon me."

Cotton Mather could take some comfort in his younger son. With other boys, Samuel met for religious discussion and prayer. His father even allowed them the use of his study for their meetings and instructed and entertained them as he could. This did not help with Cresy. "My miserable, miserable Son *Increase!* The wretch has brought himself under public Trouble and Infamy by bearing a part in a Night-Riot, with some detestable Rakes in the town."

Cotton and Increase Mather both labored and prayed with Cresy. They could not cope with the youth. In April of the next year Cotton Mather wrote in his diary, "My miserable son *Increase.* I must cast him and chase him out of my sight; forbid him to see me, until there appear sensible Marks of Repentance upon him." Cotton Mather had tried everything else. He determined finally to disown his son. "I will write a tremendous letter to my wicked Son *Increase* and after I have sett his

Crime in order before his Eyes, I will tell him that I will never own him or do for him, or look upon him, till the Characters of a Penitent are very conspicuous in him." Yet four years later Cotton Mather was still trying. "Tho' I spoke against him, yett I earnestly remember him, and my Bowels are troubled for him. Is there nothing further to be done?"

In 1716, when he was fifty-three years old, Cotton Mather married for the third time, this time Lydia Lee George, widow of a merchant. This marriage was to lead to more distressing family difficulties.

It is a relief to know that in the midst of these recurring troubles and amid his hard study and busy community life, Cotton Mather still could allow himself a little innocent recreation. In August 1716 he was prevailed upon to do something which he says he seldom did. With some gentlemen and their ladies he rode into the country for the air, and they stopped for diversion at a "famous Fish-pond." As he was getting into a canoe, Mather slipped, and he splashed into the water. Had the craft been farther from shore, he says, he would have drowned; but he clambered out, went immediately to a warm bed, and survived unharmed. With his personal life as disturbed as it was, it is little wonder that he saw the incident as a possible gloomy portent. "Am I quickly to go under the earth, as I have been under the water!"

Nine

LIKE most writers, Cotton Mather had continual trouble with his publishers. October 18, 1715, he wrote Sir William Ashurst describing conditions in Boston and in his letter said, "The Booksellers are generally such, that a celebrated Author, thinks the most opprobrious Term he can give unto them, is to say, in one word, they are Booksellers."

Publishers were bad, but Harvard was worse. It was a pain that would not go away. "Oh! for a wise, a meek, an humble, and a patient Conduct, under the Venome and Malice which the disaffected Rulers of our Colledge, treat me withal!" Because it had rejected him, Cotton Mather could only in his turn reject Harvard. He turned his back on it and looked hopefully toward the new and more orthodox Congregational college in Connecticut.

The Collegiate School of Connecticut had been founded by Congregational ministers in 1701. Torn

early by feuds and dissensions, it could not even settle
itself geographically. Started in Killingworth, it moved
to Saybrook, to Wethersfield, then in 1716 to New
Haven where it found a permanent home in a long,
narrow wooden structure built to house it. The greatest
religious and philosophical thinker in America, Jonathan
Edwards, entered as a student that year.

It was Cotton Mather who really named the college.
Striving to obtain funds and books for the struggling
college he wrote a man of wealth and position in England, January 18, 1717, "Sir, Though you have your
felicities in your family, which I pray God continue
and multiply, yet certainly if what is forming at New
Haven might wear the name of YALE COLLEGE, it
would be better than a *name of sons and daughters*. And
your munificence might easily obtain for you such a
commemoration."

Born in Boston in 1649, Elihu Yale was educated in
London. He became an official of the great East India
Company and rose to become president and governor of
Fort St. George in Madras in India, then returned to
live in England in 1699. He readily agreed to Mather's
tactfully worded proposal and made the benefactions
which changed the ministerial school in Connecticut
into Yale.

The Mathers were assiduous in trying to help the
new college. Headed by a rector who was usually absent and staffed by tutors, Yale got under way but had

hardly steadied on its course when it suffered what to it, orthodoxy, and the Mathers was a devastating blow. Yale's rector, the Reverend Timothy Cutler, who was a Harvard graduate and an ordained Congregational minister, informed the corporation that he, his two tutors, and four other ministers had decided to renounce Congregationalism and return to the Church of England. With some of the others, Cutler went to England where he was ordained an Anglican cleric. Even Harvard was shocked at what became known as the Great Apostasy. Another of the Yale "apostates" took holy orders in England, returned to this country, and some years later became the first president of King's College (Columbia) in New York.

Cotton Mather was offered the Yale presidency after Cutler's disaffection, but chose to remain where he was. As he often said thankfully, Boston was the metropolis of New England. He led one of its most important churches. He was in touch with the outer world, which he would not be on the Connecticut frontier. Jonathan Edwards returned to Yale to teach and as senior tutor —one other tutor helped instruct Yale's sixty students —became, in effect, head of the college.

As a churchman, Cotton Mather, for most of his career, was on the side of the old. As a scholar with scientific interests divorced from church organization and policy, he was just the reverse. He has been called the most advanced intellectual in the American colonies and the first to welcome and accept the new ideas of the eighteenth century.

In science he wrote on both the general and the particular. His mind was alert and receptive. In *The Christian Philosopher*, which was published in London in 1721, he tried to do what many have attempted in the centuries since his time—nothing less than to reconcile science and religion. The subject had been discussed in England but never before in the American colonies. Particularly as coming from a Puritan divine, Mather's approach and conclusions were amazingly liberal and farsighted.

In this book he wrote, "Philosophy [i.e., science] is no *Enemy* but a mighty and wondrous *Incentive* to *Religion*." He explained that the more we know, the more we must wonder at the greatness of God and in the provisions of nature. In them he found not only an indisputable argument for God's existence but also for the existence of a forgiving Christ.

Ironically, he contrasted the scientific knowledge in the Christian world with the superstition in the Mahometan. Christian thinkers acknowledge the "Shine of Heaven" through their understanding of natural phenomena, but some of the secrets revealed to Mahomet were: that wind is caused by the movement of an angel's wings; tide, by an angel's putting his foot in the middle of the ocean. Mahomet taught that falling stars are firebrands which good angels use to drive away the bad, and that thunder is the cracking of an angel's whip as he slashes the clouds to produce rain. Mather was contemptuous of "the thick-skull'd Prophet" and concluded this part of his comment by saying, *"May our Devotion exceed* the Mahometan *as much as our philosophy!"*

Mather gave separate long sections of *The Christian Philosopher* to discussions of the earth, magnetism, minerals, vegetables, and man. Under "The Vegetables" he anticipated the surgeon general of the United States and the reforming zeal of advertising copywriters and the television networks by some two hundred and fifty years.

The persuasion which Mankind has imbib'd of *Tobacco* being good for us, has in a surprizing manner prevail'd! What incredible Millions have *suck'd* in an Opinion, that it is an useful as well as a *pleasant* thing, for them to spend much of their Time in drawing thro a Pipe the *Smoke* of that lighted Weed! . . . It is to be feared that the *caustick Salt* in the *Smoke* of this Plant, convey'd by the *Salival Juice* into the blood, and also the Vellication which the continual use of it in *Snuff* gives to the *Nerves* may lay the Foundations for Diseases in Millions of unadvised People, which may be commonly and erroneously ascribed to some other Originals.

Mather's interpretation of science as an affirmation rather than a negation of religion betokened a daring intellectual position in 1721. He found no antagonism between the two, thus was able to proceed into specific scientific writing without endangering the piety which he felt and practiced so intensely.

He had read medicine as a Harvard undergraduate. There were many medical books in his father's library, and he added many more. Cotton Mather knew the medical classics of Hippocrates, Pliny, Paracelsus, and the others. He knew as well the *Religio Medici* and other writings of Sir Thomas Browne. He had medical works in languages other than English, and he had studied them.

The illnesses and deaths in his own family had intensified his interest in disease and possible cures. Many of his communications to the Royal Society concerned them. He noted that the Indians used fagiana as a cure for cancer and tried it but found it only a stimulant, like tea. He mentioned the partridge berry as a diuretic, a cordial distilled from rattlesnake gall which would induce sweating, and roots which were thought to cure jaundice.

Mather understood anatomy and physiology, the circulation of the blood, the structure of the teeth. He was acquainted with and accepted—this was extremely advanced thinking in his day—the germ theory in disease and its transmission. Almost instinctively, it would seem, he understood what the twentieth century has come to call psychosomatic medicine. Pastoral calls are often as much psychological as spiritual, and his were effective.

In his attempts to cure the supposedly possessed he had recognized the importance of diet, quiet, and of sympathetic and loving care for the disturbed.

In 1713 Cotton Mather, who had lost a wife and three children from the disease, published a pamphlet on measles. He described its symptoms and recommended moderate treatment and good nursing. Like most physicians of the eighteenth century, Cotton Mather ascribed mental illness to the Devil. He may have shared a prevailing delusion as to its cause, but the treatment he suggested was very advanced. He recommended moderate bleeding—standard medical practice for a long, long time after he wrote—but also cold drinks, bathing, exercise, reasoning, and kindness.

Cotton Mather not only thought about things medical and wrote of them, but he also tried to get something done about public health. He urged providing medical care for the poor and the retraining of practicing physicians in the newer developments in their profession. He favored medical education for women and determined to have his daughter Katy trained in "Knowledge of the Physic and the Preparation and the Dispensation of noble Medicines."

He became particularly interested in smallpox, loathsome and most dreaded disease of his and later times, feared in Europe as in America, which struck in recurring epidemics scarring its victims when it did not kill. Again, Cotton Mather had had terrible experience of the disease in his own family.

He learned of a possible preventive measure both from the Royal Society and in his own household. Because he believed that smallpox was transmitted by germs, he was convinced of the value of the method. In 1700 Dr. Martin Lister reported on inoculation for smallpox as practiced in China. The same year Dr. Clopton Havers brought inoculation to the attention of the Royal Society. Lady Mary Wortley Montagu, wife of England's ambassador to Constantinople, observed inoculation as practiced in Turkey and made it known in England. Dr. Emmanuel Timoni recommended the Turkish practice in another account. In this same year of 1716 Cotton Mather suggested a meeting of Boston physicians to consider immunization through inoculation if smallpox should strike again.

The other source of Cotton Mather's knowledge of inoculation was more homely. In 1707 a group of his parishioners in the North Church purchased a slave, Onesimus, for forty pounds and made a gift of him to their pastor for a manservant. When Cotton Mather asked him if he had ever had smallpox, Onesimus answered yes and no, and then explained what he meant in a kind of pidgin English which Mather tried to reproduce.

There has been a *wonderful practice* lately used in several parts of the world, which indeed is not yet become common in our nation.

I was first informed of it by a Garamantee servant of my own. . . . I have since met with a considerable Number of these *Africans* who all agree in one story: that in their country *grandy-mandy* dy of the *small-pox:* But now they learn this way: people take juice of *small-pox* and *cutty-skin* and put in a Drop; then by 'nd by a little sicky, sicky; then very few little things like *small-pox;* and nobody dy of it; and nobody have small-pox any more.

In 1724 Cotton Mather compiled and wrote his huge medical work. Though he used the same title for a pamphlet which was printed, the book was never published until 1953 when it appeared in abridged form as an appendix to *Cotton Mather: First Significant Figure in American Medicine* by Otho T. Beall, Jr. and Richard H. Shryock.

Mather's book, *The Angel of Bethesda*, was an ambitious undertaking, no less than an attempt to put down all that was then known and accepted in medical practice. It was to be both a textbook for physicians and a guide to medical understanding for the general public. Mentioned in John 5:2, Bethesda was a pool in Jerusalem whose waters had healing properties. Mather wished his *Angel of Bethesda* to have healing properties too.

His *Bethesda* is a pious book, for Mather believed

with his contemporaries that sin brought on a sickness of the spirit which caused sickness in the body, and that healing is of God, but it is also a full expression of the medical knowledge of the early eighteenth century and packed with Mather's informed and sensible advice. As Beall and Shryock point out, it was the only such study ever made in the English colonies of North America.

When he gave an address on "The Medical Profession in Massachusetts" before the Lowell Institute in Boston, January 29, 1869, Dr. Oliver Wendell Holmes ridiculed Cotton Mather's medical pretensions. He called *The Angel of Bethesda* (which he knew in manuscript in the American Antiquarian Society in Worcester) "a medieval work . . . running over with follies and superstitious fancies"; and the professor of anatomy and physiology at Harvard who was known principally as a wit described its author as a "meddlesome pedant."

The medical profession has never liked what it considers interference from laymen—and it was as easy for Holmes in 1869 to mock the medical beliefs and methods of the 1720's as it would be for a physician today, if he felt it necessary, to deride the medical beliefs and practices of Dr. Holmes and his fellows a century ago.

Mather's various biographers, Marvin and Beall and Shryock among them, have all pointed out with more accuracy and fairness than Holmes showed, that some of the theories Cotton Mather expounded and the remedies he prescribed were universal belief and practice when he wrote. Cotton Mather did not invent them. Because of his effort and achievement, Beall and Shryock could describe Cotton Mather, seen in perspective, as "the first significant figure in American medicine" and deserving of a place in the whole history of Western medicine.

Another of Cotton Mather's major works—the one he considered most important of all—has never been published. For many years he worked on a huge compilation of what amounted to small sermons which would illustrate particular Scriptural texts and passages. What he intended, he said when he began his *Biblia Americana*, was a great commentary which would give more material than any existing Bible commentary offered. By 1706 the manuscript was already twice as long as his large *Magnalia*. He announced his forthcoming book that year. It was finished and existed in six large manuscript folios by 1712. A prospectus of the tremendous work was issued some years later, and there is a four-page advertisement for it in the back of Samuel Mather's life of his father which was published in 1729. The *Biblia Americana* was to be sold by subscription, three volumes for between three and four pounds sterling. The book is still in manuscript in the Massachusetts Historical Society in Boston.

Mather did much of all this work under difficulties

which must sometimes have sent him nearly distracted. There were disputes and unpleasantness with many of his relatives. His first wife's brother was Cotton Mather's outspoken enemy. A John Oliver married Mather's sister Hannah when she was seventeen and seems to have mistreated her. Cotton Mather attended his sister faithfully in 1706 when she was incurably ill and repeatedly called for him. Not until after her death did the husband praise his wife, saying brokenly that she had been good, and change his attitude toward Cotton Mather. Three of Mather's sisters were widowed and principally dependent upon him for financial support. One after another his children sickened and died. In 1721 when he was deep in controversy and mercilessly bedeviled by his adversaries, his daughter Nibby ("my Lovely Nibby") was dying in childbirth and her father went to her daily.

With his father aging and ill, most of the work of the Second Church fell on the son. On his eightieth birthday Increase Mather preached on "The Day when thou wast born" from Ezekiel 16:5. In late September 1722 he suffered an apoplectic stroke and never left his home again. The aged man was taken with fits of hiccoughing and suffered intensely. His mind was affected and his speech incoherent. The son who had worked with him so closely for so many years was constantly in attendance. On the day he knew he was dying, Increase Mather sent for him again, and Cotton Mather did what he could to comfort him and ease his own grief.

Cotton Mather said that his father suffered a martyr's death during the torment of his last three weeks. At the very last he said to the dying old man, *"Sir, the Messenger is come to tell you, This Day shalt thou be with me in Paradise; Do you believe it, Sir, and rejoice in the Views and Hopes of it?"* Increase Mather gasped, "I do! I do! I do!" and died in his sons's arms.

Seven days later Massachusetts Bay gave the Rev. Dr. Increase Mather, who was virtually the father of the province, almost a state funeral. The lieutenant governor, Chief Justice Samuel Sewall, the president of Harvard, and three leading ministers served as pallbearers. Some sixty other ministers and one hundred and sixty Harvard students followed the casket. A vast crowd looked on as the procession wended its way through the streets of Boston. The Reverend Thomas Foxcroft, one of Increase Mather's friends, gave the funeral sermon. He took his text from 2 Chronicles 24:15–16: "He was full of days when he died, and they buried him honourably, because he had done good in Israel."

Ten

I N SEPTEMBER 1841 Nathaniel Hawthorne had an idea for another story about Puritan New England. In his notebook he wrote, ". . . Cotton Mather . . . walking the streets of Boston, and lifting up his hands to bless the people, while they all revile him. An old dame should be seen, flinging water or emptying some vials of medicine on his head from the latticed window of an old-fashioned house; and all around must be tokens of pestilence and mourning,— as a coffin borne along,—and a woman and children weeping on a doorstep. Can the tolling of the Old South bell be painted?"

In 1721 Cotton Mather was even more hated in Boston than Hawthorne imagined. He was condemned in public and in the press. Enraged mobs attacked his house. A determined attempt was made to murder him.

In mid-April of that year a ship from the Tortugas in the West Indies brought more than its cargo and crew to Boston. It brought the smallpox. The disease swept swiftly through the town and reached epidemic proportion in May. People were dead and dying everywhere. It was just such a situation as Cotton Mather had envisioned and for which he had suggested preventive measures five years before.

He wrote and, June 6, 1721, circulated in manuscript "An Address to the Physicians of Boston." In it he urged inoculation of those not yet stricken. He quoted the reports from Turkey, described the methods used, advised that the inoculating be done with great care and only by skilled physicians.

Mather, who knew that smallpox was germ-carried and that millions of germs were found in the pustules when viewed through a microscope, called the dread disease, "more an animalculated business than we have generally been aware of." June 24 he wrote Dr. Zabdiel Boylston, "If upon mature deliberation you should think it advisiable [sic] to be proceeded in, inoculation may save many lives that we set a great value on."

Born in 1679, Zabdiel Boylston was the son of Dr. Thomas Boylston, the first physician in Brookline. He studied medicine with his father and with Dr. Cutter in Boston, where he began successful practice and quickly became known for his skill, humanity, and watchful care of his patients. Boylston was convinced by Cotton Mather's arguments. June 26, 1721, he inoculated his son Thomas and then two slaves, who thus became the first persons ever inoculated for smallpox in America. Later he inoculated another son, John, and on July 21 another seven patients. Boylston was the only Boston physician who dared the experiment.

The other Boston physicians joined in a vicious attack on Cotton Mather and Zabdiel Boylston. They were led by Dr. William Douglass, with whom Mather had been friendly and who had actually lent Mather reports dealing with inoculation in other parts of the world. A Scotsman who had studied medicine in Edinburgh, Leyden, and Paris, Douglass was a newcomer in Boston, to which he had come after a stay in the West Indies in 1718. He had the prestige of a medical degree, though it is not known where in Europe he had obtained it. As there were no medical schools in the colonies to grant degrees, most of his colleagues had none.

Boylston announced in the Boston *Gazette* that all of his inoculations had been successful and that shortly he would make public specific results. Boston's other doctors replied angrily in the *Boston News-Letter*, July 24, 1721, that inoculation was dangerous and irreligious. The leading Boston ministers, including Benjamin Colman and Increase Mather, who was still alive, supported inoculation in the *Gazette* for July 31. They contended that inoculation was no worse in the sight of God than bleeding, blistering, and other acceptable practices. The irony has been pointed out that the physicians attacked inoculation on religious grounds while the ministers defended it on scientific.

Douglass denounced Boylston as having no medical degree and "Mather, jr.," as he called him, for being no physician at all but a dangerously ignorant layman. Mather wrote, and he and Boylston circulated a pamphlet in their defense. While people lay dead and dying a fierce pamphlet warfare raged. Mather wrote "An Account of the Method and Success of Inoculating the Small-pox in New England" and his "Little Treatise on the Small-pox." He defended inoculation, Boylston, and himself.

Boston's enraged doctors were not content with words. Three times they had Dr. Boylston hauled before the Boston Selectmen and judges. Boylston was forbidden to proceed with the inoculating. He went ahead anyway. Always a fighter, Cotton Mather did more than speak and write too. He was visiting and trying to comfort the stricken everywhere. He feared for his own family. If he did not have his children inoculated, he might be responsible for their deaths; if he did and the inoculations failed or were made too late, he would be accused of murdering them. He was himself in continual danger of violence through the public opposition which the doctors had aroused. "They rave, they rail, they blaspheme," he wrote in his diary, "they talk not only like idiots, but also like franticks. Not only the physician who began the experiment, but I also am the object of their fury. . . ."

His son Samuel begged to have his life saved by inoculation, and the father had the operation performed. Samuel grew so violently ill that it was feared he had contracted the disease before immunization. He developed such a high fever that it appeared he could not live, but the fever broke, and he recovered. Two of Mather's daughters were very ill and appeared to be dying. Another daughter, Abigail, and her husband were very ill. Abigail and her newborn child both died. The son, daughter, and grandson of one of Mather's sisters all had smallpox. Mather went about praying with the sick and bereaved. One day he led thirty-seven such prayers. He was so exhausted he thought he might himself be fatally stricken.

Cotton Mather brought a young ministerial kinsman from Roxbury to his own house for the inoculation he asked. This was in November 1721 when the outcry against him was at its height. In his diary he wrote again, "This abominable Town, treats me in a most malicious and murderous manner, for my doing as CHRIST would have me do, in saving the Lives of the People from an horrible Death; but I will go on, in the imitation of my admirable SAVIOUR, and overcome Evil with good." He was determined and knew that his efforts had been vindicated. "The sottish Errors and cursed Clamours, that fill the Town and the Countrey, raging against the astonishing *Success* of the Small-pox Inoculated; make it seasonable for me, to state the Case, and exhibit that which may silence the unreasonable People."

Mather did not exaggerate the mob's fury. He gave his own bedroom to his kinsman after the young minister had been inoculated. Ignorant of this, someone, about three o'clock of the morning of November 14, hurled a bomb (a "granado") into the room where the Roxbury minister was sleeping. An iron ball, sufficient in itself to kill if it struck a man's head, was packed with gunpowder and a mixture of turpentine and other inflammatory materials. Had it exploded, it would have killed everyone in the house and probably, as Mather said, speedily have laid the house itself in ashes. But, *"this night there stood by me the Angel of God, whose I am and whom I serve. . . ."*

The fuse of the bomb struck the metal casing of the window and was broken loose before it could fire the bomb. On the fuse, so attached that it would survive explosion of the shell, was a written message: *"COTTON MATHER, You Dog, Dam you; I'll inoculate you with this, with a Pox to you."*

The authorities offered a reward of fifty pounds for apprehension of the criminal but never had to pay it. Instead, Mather said he had proofs that people applauded the bombing and promised that a new attempt "shall doe the Business more effectually." Bitterly he wrote in his diary:

I have been guilty of such a Crime as this. I have communi-cated a never-failing and most allowable Method, of pre-venting Death and other grievous miseries by a terrible Distemper, among my Neighbors. Every day demonstrates that if I had been hearken'd to, many precious Lives (many Hundred) had been saved. The Opposition to it has been carried on with senseless Ignorance and raging Wickedness.

The facts proved how right Cotton Mather was. Crowds had fled the infected city. Of those who re-mained about one-half, 5,889, got the smallpox in 1721, and 884 of them died. Dr. Zabdiel Boylston inoculated 242 patients. Of these only six died, and it is likely that they had already been infected.

James and Benjamin Franklin, who was only sixteen years old at the time, fought inoculation and the Math-ers in their *New England Courant*, but Franklin later changed his mind and approved inoculation. It took Dr. William Douglass, a man of strong prejudices, thirty years before he would admit publicly that he too had changed his mind. Dr. Zabdiel Boylston was thoroughly vindicated. He spent two years, 1724–1726, in London where he lectured before the Royal College of Physi-cians and published *An Historical Account of the Small-pox inoculated in New England*. As tough-fibered as Cotton Mather was convinced and indomitable, he returned to his Boston practice. After he retired to breed horses on his Brookline farm, he was seen breaking a colt when he was eighty-four years old.

Cotton Mather's major accomplishment in preventive medicine cannot be minimized—nor can the impulses which underlie his achievement. His thirst for knowledge could never be slaked, and, no snob, he sought facts where he could find them and appraised them on both the basis of wide learning and human understanding. He combined scientific findings with his trust in the words and experience of Onesimus, the slave. Despite raging opposition from the powerfully entrenched, he applied what he learned for the benefit of his fellows in another of his own unceasing essays to do good. Though vaccination has succeeded inoculation for smallpox, the principle he understood and the practice he established in this country remain in force.

Eleven

COTTON MATHER tried another experiment in 1722. He invited his disowned Increase to live at home again, and Increase, who was now twenty-two years old, came. Evidently this experiment was not successful, for this time Increase left both home and Boston. In the summer of 1724 Mather learned that his son had been lost at sea. The ship in which he had sailed from the Barbados was not reported five months after it left port.

"Oh! My Son Increase! My Son! My Son!" Mather wrote brokenly in his diary. A month later there was a rumor that Increase was still alive, but the rumor proved false. In September, Cotton Mather preached a sermon on his son's death. He published it toward the end of the year, "that the Child, who did so little Good, but much ill, all the Days of his Life, may do some Good at his death. . . ."

He was grateful that his younger son, Samuel, gained

the uncommon honor of an M.A. at Yale in September 1724 when he was not yet eighteen years old but was already esteemed as a preacher. Cotton Mather needed all the consolation he could get at this time, for he suffered a new domestic crisis.

His wife went insane, at least became severely disturbed, and turned violently upon him. To Mather she seemed to suffer something "little short of a proper Satanical Possession." Rousing him at midnight with a thousand curses, she screamed that she would never live with him or stay in his house again. She called a niece and her maid and stormed over to a neighbor's house demanding sanctuary.

Lydia George Mather ranted and raved against her husband, giving wild expression to her hatred and contempt for him. The shocked and sorrowing Mather felt that she took every means to ruin his public esteem and the success of his ministry. "GOD knows," he declared passionately, "that she has no manner of Reason to treat me in the Manner that she does." Almost pitifully he wrote of ". . . my Consort's leaving of my Bed, when I am a Person of whom there cannot be the least Pretence of my being a Person universally acceptable."

His wife returned to her home and, seemingly, to her senses. She came back begging her husband's forgiveness and harmony in their relations. Though she had no children of her own, Lydia Mather had the respect and affection of Mather's remaining children by his earlier marriages as well as Mather's, but her mental and nervous instability made life hard.

In 1716 Cotton Mather had written in an upsurge of grateful emotion, "My heart is exceedingly affected with the most comfortable and undeserved Enjoyments in my Domestic Circumstances. I can scarce desire to be better off, than I am, upon all accounts. An aimiable Consort, agreeable children, most accommodated Habitation, a plentiful Table, the Respects of Kind Neighbors, a flourishing Auditory. . . ." He still had the flourishing auditory, but most of the other blessings he had been so thankful for eight years earlier were fled.

Fortunately for Cotton Mather his real life was in his mind. His real home was his library which grew to contain between two and three thousand books. He never ceased to grow. As his interests widened, he became more tolerant. Determinedly orthodox in his earlier years, he became more liberal both in precept and in practice. He admitted Baptists, Presbyterians, and men and women of other denominations to membership in his church. In 1726 he published another of his most useful and influential books. Its title describes both its contents and its purpose.

Manductio ad Ministerium or Directions for a Candidate of the Ministry. Wherein, FIRST, a Right FOUNDATION is laid for his Future Improvement; And, Then, RULES are offered for such a Management of his *Academ-*

ical & Preparatory STUDIES; And, Thereupon, For such a CONDUCT after his APPEARANCE in the World; as may Render him a SKILFUL and USEFUL MINISTER OF THE GOSPEL. . . . Boston. Printed for Thomas Hancock, and Sold at his Shop in Ann-Street, near the Draw Bridge, 1726.

The *Manductio* is a sensible small book from which generations of ministers have profited. Mather discussed worship, logic, languages, ethics, natural philosophy, mathematics, music, even geography. The book ends with a list of twenty "Rules of Prudence." Don't tell all you know. Don't spend all you have. Think before you speak. Bridle your tongue. Avoid centention. Don't quarrel. Ignore your adversaries and write useful books. Have a wise and good person for a friend—but don't tell him everything. Lay up an inexhaustible store of good stories. Be thoughtful and prayerful.

Rules nineteen and twenty bear witness to Cotton Mather's shrewdness, common sense, and—what he is too seldom credited with—his sense of humor.

XIX. It may not be amiss for you to have *Two Heaps. An heap* of UNINTELLIGIBLES; and *an heap* of INCURABLES. Every now and then you will meet with something or other, that may pretty well distress your Thoughts; But the *shortest Way* with the Vexations will be, *To throw them into the heap they belong to* and be no more distressed about them.

XX. 'Tis a Trespass on the *Rules of Prudence*, not to know, *when to have done. Wherefore, I have done!*

That was his sound conclusion to the practical little book in which, among so many other things, he discussed style in writing. He had a right to describe it, for he was a working writer. He had written hundreds of sermons, histories, biographies, scientific papers, medical books, polemical arguments, political fables, poetry—and he had written in a variety of styles. He had written ornate prose, all fantasy and flourishes, filled with allusions to Greek and Roman works and to contemporary writing in many languages. At the other extreme, he had been as hard, simple, and direct as a writer can be.

Like most hard-working writers, Cotton Mather had little use for critics. "The Blades that set up for *Criticks*, I know not who constituted or commissioned 'em!— they appear to me for the most part as *Contemptible*, as they are a *Supercilious* Generation." Mather praised poetry and condemned too many plays for their immoral passages, Then, sensibly, he decided, "After all, Every Man will have his own *Style*, which will distinguish him as much as his gate [gait]. . . . I wonder what ails People, that they can't let *Cicero* write in the *Style of Cicero* and *Seneca* write in the (much other!) *style of Seneca.* . . ."

Mather's own style was flexible. He could use the

very literary as in his *Magnalia*, with conscious artistry suiting what he considered a noble style to a noble subject. In his *Bonifacius* he had been simple, direct, almost slangy. He is as simple in the *Manductio*, but more relaxed—a man in charge of his subject. Sensitive to changes in literary as well as in religious and scientific thought, Mather wrote with less elaboration in his later work, but he always made matter and manner merge. Whatever he wrote and in whatever way, he wrote clearly. This was not a matter of consciously adopted style. Mather's writing is always lucid because his mind was clear. That was his distinguishing gait.

In the *Manductio* Mather told (clearly and forcefully) which style he liked and why he preferred it. It was the style he had used in his *Magnalia*. "There is a *way of writing* wherein the Author endeavors that the reader may have *something to the Purpose* in every Paragraph. There is not only a *vigour* sensible in every *Sentence*, but the Paragraph is embellish'd with *Profitable References*, even to something beyond what is *directly spoken*. Formal and Painful *quotations* are not studied, yet all that could be heard from them is insinuated. The Writer pretends not unto *Reading*, yet he could not have writ as he does if he had not Read very much in his Time, and his Composures are not only *Cloth of Gold*, but also stuck with as many *Jewels* as the Gown of a Russian Ambassador."

Cotton Mather was a skilled professional writer who

knew his trade thoroughly. He could indulge in convoluted rhetorical flourishes or he could go straight to the point. His observations were often trenchant or ironic. As with many sound writers, his practice was better than his theory.

In *Winter Meditations*, which he published in Boston in 1693, he described the cold in Boston as fierce and hard but pleasant and wholesome. Most winter days were fair—"not such dirty, sloppy, lowering things as fill the winters in some other lands." How, he asked, best employ them? "To sleep all winter more befits a bear than a man." Work for God, he suggested. Use the long winter to read the Bible. He grew sharp. "I do confess that I have written too many books for one of my small attainments, and I would say to my reader, whom I now suppose by the fireside, if this or any book of mine hinder men from acquainting themselves with the Bible, I wish, as Luther did about his own books, that they were all thrown into the fire."

This sounds like spoken language. It was. Mather first gave his *Winter Meditations* at a Boston lecture in December 1692. Probably his audience smiled when, referring to his own writing, he quoted a Roman writer who said, " 'I expect nothing but only to be frost-bitten with envy for what I do.' " Mather could turn a phrase to his own use.

He could and did rap Boston over its chapped knuckles for its sins. Houses of ill repute should be smoked out, he declared in "The Boston Ebenezer," which he gave April 7, 1698. "And, Oh! that the drinking houses in the town might come under a laudable *regulation*. . . . When once a man is bewitched with the ordinary [tavern], what usually becomes of him? He is a gone man; and when he comes to die, he will cry out, as many have done, 'Ale-houses are hell-houses! ale-houses are hell-houses!' "

The reformer could turn then and become the storyteller in fast-paced narration of adventure. Mather's *Life of His Excellency Sir William Phips*, etc. is a eulogistic account which reads like the campaign biographies which were a feature of American life all through the nineteenth century, and in the twentieth too. Hawthorne wrote one for Franklin Pierce, and William Dean Howells wrote one for Abraham Lincoln. Both these writers were rewarded with lucrative consular posts abroad. Others who performed similar literary chores were paid by offices, but Phips was dead when Mataher's book appeared in London in 1697. Anti-Mather critics accused Cotton Mather of using the book as propaganda to justify his partisanship, but it does not read that way. It reads like a novel.

The *Life* is fulsome in its praise of the ship's carpenter who rose to knighthood and a royal governorship, but it is also a sturdy narrative, a swift-moving story of sunken treasure, mutiny, and attempted marooning.

The rags-to-riches story is combined with the adventure tale.

Mather does not waste a word in his account of the central action. The Spanish galleon had been located. The divers had been going down, but they found nothing. Hard-bitten Phips and his hard-bitten crew were discouraged. Then one Indian diver brought up a "sow," or lump of silver, worth two or three hundred pounds. Saying nothing, the crew slipped it to one side of the table when they talked with their captain.

At last he *saw* it; seeing it, he cried out with some Agony, Why? *What is this? Whence comes this?* And then, with changed Countenance they told him *how*, and *where* they got it. Then, said he, *Thanks be to God! We are made;* and so away they went, all hands to Work. . . . Now, most happily, they fell upon that Room in the *Wreck*, where the *Bullion* had been stored up; and they so prospered in this *New Fishery*, that in a little while they had, without the loss of any Man's life, brought up *Thirty Two Tuns* of Silver; for it was now come to measuring of Silver by *Tuns*. . . . Thus did there once again come into the Light of the Sun, a Treasure which had been half an Hundred Years groaning under the Waters; and in this time there was grown upon the Plate, a Crust like *Limestone* to the thickness of several Inches; which Crust being broken open by Irons contrived for that purpose, they knockt out whole Bushels of rusty Pieces of Eight which were grown thereinto. Besides that incredible Treasure of Plate in various forms, thus fetch'd up, from Seven or Eight Fathoms under Water, there were vast Riches of *Gold*, and *Pearls*, and *Jewels*, which they also lit upon; and indeed, for a more Comprehensive *Invoice*, I must but summarily say, *All that* a Spanish *Frigot uses to be enricht withal.*

Cotton Mather could tell a story. He could also be a graphic reporter. February 28, 1717, he noted "an horrid storm" in his diary. December 10, 1717, he made that storm the subject of a long letter to Dr. John Woodward. He knew that, like him, Woodward and the Royal Society would be especially interested in the survival of animals in cold and without food for long periods, and this item in his *Curiosa Americana* centers on that interest, but it is also a blizzard made real. You can feel the cold and the darkness in houses buried under the snow, the loneliness and the silence, shudder at the deaths of animals trapped in deep drifts. You know it once snowed in Boston.

On the Twentieth of the last *February*, there came on a *Snow*, which being added unto what had covered the ground a few Days before, made a Thicker Mantle for our Mother [earth] than what was usual; And the Storm with it, was for the following Day so violent, as to make all communications between the Neighbors every where to cease. People for some Hours could not pass from one side of a Street unto another. . . . But on the Twenty-fourth Day of the Month comes *Pelion* upon Ossa. Another *Snow* came on, which almost buried the Memory of the former; with a Storm so furious that Heaven laid an interdict on the Religious Assemblies throughout the countrey on this Lords-day, the like whereunto had never been seen before. The Indians near an hundred years old, affirm that their Fathers never told them of any thing that equall'd it. Vast Numbers of Cattel were destroy'd in this Calamity; Whereof some that were of the Strongest Sort, were found standing Dead on their Legs, as if they had been alive, many weeks after, when the Snow melted away. And others had their Eyes glazed over with Ice at such a rate, that not being far from the Sea, they went out of their way, and drowned them there.

One Gentleman, on whose Farms, there were now Lost above eleven hundred *Sheep*, which with other cattel were Interred (Shall I say, or Inniv'd) in the Snow; writes me that there were Two *Sheep* in very singularly circumstances. For no less than Eight & Twenty Days after the Storm, the people pulling out the Ruines of above an hundred Sheep, out of a Snow-bank, which lay sixteen foot high drifted over them, there were Two found alive, which had been there all this time, & kept themselves alive by Eating the Wool of their Dead Companions. When they were taken out, they shed their own Fleeces, but soon got into good Case again.

Mather went on to tell of hogs and poultry given up for dead which survived under the snow without food, some for three or four weeks. Deer and foxes came out of the woods, struggling toward the shore. Great flocks of sparrows appeared, then vanished. Orchards were severely damaged as animals walking on the snow crusted twelve feet above ground ate the tops and upper branches of the trees. Many were split by the weight of the ice and snow. "The Ocean was in a prodigious Ferment, and after it was over, Vast Heaps of Little Shells were driven ashore, where there were never any seen before. Mighty Shoals of Porpoises, also kept a Play-day in the Disturbed Waves of our Harbours."

Mather wrote that there were many strange stories about people whose cottages, even their chimney tops, were buried in the horrid snow, but because, as he said, these were without scientific interest, he forbore relating them. He said he wished a thousand times during the storm and its aftermath that he were with Dr. Woodward in Gresham College, "which is never so horribly Snowd's upon." He signed himself, "Syr, Yours with an Affection that knows no Winter."

Twelve

AFTER the death of his father, Cotton Mather
was the senior pastor of the Second Church. A
younger man, the Reverend Joshua Gee, was made his
associate, but Mather was the responsible head of the
church. He was increasingly busy with its management
and with his preaching. Some years he preached as many
as sixty sermons, many of them later published. He
called on the sick, looked after the needy, kept up his
wide correspondence, engaged in private prayer many
times a day, and worked unremittingly in his study.
He spoke at midweek lectures and preached at funerals.

One funeral at which he preached in August of 1726
was that of Mrs. Elizabeth Cooper. She was Cotton
Mather's twenty-two-year-old daughter Elizabeth. For
the thirteenth time he saw one of his children to the
grave.

In April 1727 Cotton Mather was so seriously ill that
other ministers gathered to pray for his recovery. Ill-

ness never slowed him longer than he could help. As quickly as he was well, he was hard at it again. He sent sermon after sermon to the press in 1727, and soon he found unusual opportunity for his ministerial work.

About eleven o'clock of the night of October 29, 1727, Boston experienced an earthquake. A first marked shock was followed by several others of lesser intensity. It was not a major upheaval, but it was at least a surprise. As Cotton Mather described it, ". . . there was heard in Boston, passing from one end of the town to the other, a horrid rumbling like the noise of many coaches together driving on the paved stones with the upmost rapidity." Houses rocked and swayed. Chimneys tumbled. Bricks and stones crashed down. China fell and was smashed in the houses; books and pictures fell, and pots and pans rattled. There were strange flames of light in the sky. The populace was fearful and aghast.

The next morning, when it was all over, the bells of the Old North rang, and people rushed to service. The ministers of Boston's churches spoke there to a crowd that filled the city's largest church and pressed outside. The following Tuesday was a lecture day. Governor Jeremiah Dummer directed that it be made a day of supplication and thanksgiving for deliverance from threatened destruction.

Cotton Mather spoke then about the earthquake, about earthquakes in other places, about those in Biblical times, and—being the man he was—on the natural causes of earthquakes. He exhorted his listeners to repentance in this sermon which, when published, went quickly through several editions. To reinforce the impression which it made, he followed this in December with an essay, "Boanerges."

New England was beginning to experience a series of revivals, known then as "awakenings." Touched off by Jonathan Edwards in Northampton, about one hundred miles west of Boston in the Connecticut Valley, in 1733, they would culminate in the Great Awakening which swept through Massachusetts towns, villages, and countryside in the 1740's. The Reverend Eleazar Mather, brother of Increase, thus Cotton Mather's uncle, had been Northampton's first minister. In 1727 Cotton Mather saw the beginning of these awakenings which brought more than the ordinary number to membership in his church that year. He rejoiced in the new spirit of religion now manifest.

In December he preached a funeral sermon for an aged friend, Peter Thatcher, who had died on the seventeenth of the month, and sent it to the press. Then he fell ill again.

"My *last Enemy* is come. I would say my *Last Friend*," he told his son and biographer, Samuel Mather. Cotton Mather was ill for five or six weeks. As he lay dying, the son asked him for his last word. Cotton Mather gave it. "Remember only that one word, *Fructuosus*." Fruitful was just what he had been. Richard

Mather had lived to be seventy-five, and Increase Mather to be eighty-four. Cotton Mather died the day after his sixty-fifth birthday, February 13, 1728.

He had worked hard as a minister, a historian, a biographer, a scientist, and a social reformer. He had worn himself out with his own intensity. Cotton Mather was very much alive while he lived—which in itself, perhaps, is a way of praising God, the end toward which he had devoted all his strength and abilities.

Once more there was a great Mather funeral. There were the crowds and the eulogies. The lieutenant governor and other dignitaries of the Province of Massachusetts Bay, the governor's council, the House of Representatives, many ministers, judges, merchants, other prominent men, and Harvard students followed the coffin through streets filled with spectators, while others watched sorrowfully from the windows of their homes.

Though, aged seventy-eight, he was forced to ride in his coach, Judge Samuel Sewall was one of the pallbearers. Another was the Reverend Benjamin Colman of Brattle Street. The Reverend Joshua Gee gave the funeral sermon. Burial was in the Mather tomb in the northeast corner of the old Copp's Hill Burying Ground.

On the day of the funeral, February 19, 1728, the *New England Weekly Journal* said that Cotton Mather "was, perhaps, the principal ornament of this country, and the greatest scholar that ever was bred in it." The press which had so often struck at him felt differently about him now. His friend and associate of more than a quarter century, Benjamin Colman, said that Cotton Mather had been *"The first minister in the town;* the first in age, in gifts, and in grace . . . the first in the whole Province, and Providence of New England, for universal literature, and extensive services. Yes, it may be among all the *fathers* in these churches, from the beginning of this Country to this day. . . ."

Pastor of the Old South, Dr. Thomas Prince spoke with awe of Cotton Mather. "Great abilities, an insatiable thirst for all kinds of knowledge, an extraordinary quickness of apprehension, liveliness of fancy, with a ready invention and active spirit seem to be the chief ingredients of his natural genius. . . ." Prince described Cotton Mather too as "an utter enemy to religious tyranny and impositions."

De mortuis nil nisi bonum, of course, but there was more than that. With warm sincerity and a sense of deep loss, the men who knew Cotton Mather best praised him for his character and achievements and for the qualities which they knew he had—generosity and tolerance. They considered him an admirable man.

Stridently announced by self-assured critics ("I know not who constituted or commissioned 'em"), moral judgments of many kinds are as characteristic of the late twentieth century in the United States as belief in witches was in the American colonies of the late seventeenth. Thus one more may not be impertinent. Like most men, he had his faults, but the Reverend Cotton Mather, D.D., F.R.S., was an honest servant of God and those he always called his neighbors.

Bibliography

Beall, Otho T., Jr., and Shryock, Richard H. "Cotton Mather: First Significant Figure in American Medicine," *Proceedings, American Antiquarian Society*, Vol. 63, 1953.

Calef, Robert. *More Wonders of the Invisible World.* Reproduced from the London edition of 1700 in *Salem Witchcraft*, ed., Samuel P. Fowler. Salem: H. P. Ives and A. A. Smith, 1861.

Holmes, Oliver Wendell. "The Medical Profession in Massachusetts," *Medical Essays*, Vol. 9, *Holmes's Works*. Boston and New York: Houghton, Mifflin Co., 1892.

Holmes, Thomas J. "The Mather Collection at Cleveland," *The Colophon*, Pt. 14, 1933.

————, *The Mather Literature*. Cleveland: Privately printed for William Gwynn Mather, 1927.

Kittredge, George Lyman, "Cotton Mather's Scientific Communications to the Royal Society," *Proceedings, American Antiquarian Society*, New Series, Vol. 26, 1916.

The Life of the late Reverend and Learned Dr. Cotton Mather of Boston, (New England). Prefatory Recommendation by Isaac Watts dated Newington near London, August 13,

1743. Philadelphia: American Sunday School Union, n.d.

Marvin, Rev. Abijah P. *The Life and Times of Cotton Mather, D.D., F.R.S., or a Boston Minister of Two Centuries Ago, 1663–1728.* Boston and Chicago: Congregational Sunday School and Publishing Society, 1892.

Mather, Cotton. *Boanerges.* A Short Essay to preserve and strengthen the Good Impressions produced by Earthquakes on the Minds of People that have been AWAKENED with them. Boston: printed for S. Kneeland, and sold at his Shop in *King Street,* 1727.

——, *Bonifacius, An Essay Upon the Good.* London: 1710. Also Cambridge: Belknap Press of Harvard University Press, 1966.

——, *Diary of Cotton Mather.* Preface by Worthington Chauncey Ford. New York: Frederick Ungar Publishing Co., n.d. (from same, Boston: The Massachusetts Historical Society, 1811–1912).

——, *Diary of Cotton Mather, D.D., F.R.S., for the year 1712,* ed. with intro. and notes by William R. Manierre, II. Charlottesville: The University of Virginia Press, 1964.

——, *Magnalia Christi Americana;* or the Ecclesiastical History of New England from its first planting in the Year 1620 Unto the Year of Our Lord, 1698. London: Printed for Thomas Parkhurst at the Bible and Three Crowns in Cheapside, near Mercers Chapel, 1807. Also, 2 vol. Hartford: Silus Andrus, 1820.

——, *Manductio ad Ministerium.* Bibliographic notes by Thomas J. Holmes and Kenneth B. Murdock. New York: Columbia University Press, 1938.

——, *The Wonders of the Invisible World.* London, 1693. Reproduced in *Salem Witchcraft,* ed. Samuel P. Fowler, 1861.

Mather, Samuel. *The Life of the Very Reverend and Learned Cotton Mather, D.D. and F.R.S.* Boston in New England: Printed for Samual Gerrish, 1729.

Memoirs of the Life of the Late Reverend Increase Mather. Preface by the Reverend Edmund Calamy, D.D. London: printed for John Clarke and Richard Hett at the Bible and Crown in the Poultry, 1725.

Miller, Perry. *The New England Mind,* the Seventeenth Century. Cambridge: Harvard University Press, 1954.

————, ed. *The American Puritans, their Prose and Poetry.* Garden City: Doubleday and Co., 1956.

Murdock, Kenneth Ballard. *Increase Mather, The Foremost American Puritan.* Cambridge: Harvard University Press, 1926.

————, "Cotton Mather," "Increase Mather," "Richard Mather," in *Dictionary of American Biography*, Cent. Ed. New York: Charles Scribner's Sons, 1946.

————, ed. *Selections from Cotton Mather.* New York: Harcourt, Brace and Co., 1926.

Peabody, William Bourn Oliver. *Cotton Mather.* Vol. VI, The Library of American Biography conducted by Jared Sparks. New York: Harper & Bros., 1836.

Schneider, Herbert Wallace. *The Puritan Mind.* New York: Henry Holt and Co., 1930.

Starkey, Marion L. *The Devil in Massachusetts,* A Modern Enquiry into the Salem Witch Trials. New York: Alfred Knopf, Inc., 1949.

Trent, William P., and Wells, Benjamin W., eds. *Colonial Literature.* Second Series. New York: Thomas Y. Crowell & Son, 1903.

Wendell, Barrett. *Cotton Mather, the Puritan Priest.* New York: Dodd, Mead, and Co., 1891.

Wood, James Playsted. *Boston.* New York: The Seabury
    Press, 1967.
————, *Mr. Jonathan Edwards.* New York: The Seabury
    Press, 1968.

Index